# BIBLE CALLING

# Bible Calling

## NORAH FREED
on Trans-World Radio from Monte Carlo

LONDON

LUTTERWORTH PRESS

*First published* 1968

COPYRIGHT © 1968 NORAH FREED

*London: Lutterworth Press, 4 Bouverie Street, E.C.4*

7188 1414 2

*Printed in Great Britain*
*by Richard Clay (The Chaucer Press), Ltd., Bungay, Suffolk*

# Contents

| | Page |
|---|---|
| THE POTTER | 7 |
| THE SHUNAMMITE (1) | 9 |
| THE SHUNAMMITE (2) | 12 |
| THE ETERNAL HOME | 14 |
| SHORT CUTS! | 17 |
| FORGIVENESS | 20 |
| EMERGENCIES | 22 |
| A BROKEN CONFIDENCE | 25 |
| HONOURING GOD | 28 |
| KNITTING | 31 |
| JONAH REBELLIOUS | 33 |
| JONAH REMORSEFUL | 36 |
| JONAH RECOMMISSIONED | 38 |
| JONAH RESENTFUL | 41 |
| ADORNMENT | 43 |
| TELEPHONES | 46 |
| FRET NOT! | 48 |
| CORNERS OF THE WAY | 51 |
| DOWN IN THE VALLEY | 54 |
| SPOT OR WRINKLE | 56 |
| I FORGOT | 59 |
| FORGETTING MY TOIL | 61 |
| BUT GOD | 64 |
| MIRACLES | 66 |
| PENINNAH THE PROVOKER | 68 |
| CRITICISM | 70 |
| SHUT IN | 72 |
| BIRTHDAYS | 75 |

# THE POTTER

"The vessel was marred . . . so He made it
again." *Jeremiah 18:4*

Not long ago I was sitting in the dentist's chair having a tooth filled. Suddenly, he stopped the drill and said, "Mrs. Freed, relax your tongue. That's better," and he started the drill again. You know, I was so taut, waiting every moment lest that thing would touch a spot and hurt, that I had not realized that I was offering resistance and hindering him in the very thing he was trying to do for me! Actually, the moment of pain never did come! If you have had that type of work done on your teeth, I am sure you know just what I mean. Maybe you have felt as I did that morning. I think it is always a fact that fear of things hurting builds up a tension inside, but what relief when one is able to relax and the strain goes!

The same thing applies in our spiritual lives, doesn't it? I have just been recalling the day we visited a potter's house in Jerusalem. We were a bit early for him that morning, but the owner was very gracious when he knew we were limited for time and allowed his chief workman to show us how they worked. There was the lump of clay: nothing very pretty about it, but he put it on the board and began to knead it well, just like you would the dough for a loaf. Backwards and forwards, over and over, pressure on pressure until it was smooth and supple in his hands, relaxed and easy to work with.

There was my first lesson, taking me back to that story in Jeremiah 18. Clay in the hands of the potter. Clay without any pretentious ambitions to be something other than the master desired, yielding to his touch, ready to be shaped and moulded as he wished. Can you fit yourself into that picture? I asked the potter why so much hard kneading was necessary, and he said, "To make sure the clay is ready before I begin to shape it." Doesn't that answer some of the questions you are asking about the Lord's dealings? As I looked on, I remembered words I had often sung,

7

"Be thou the skilful Potter and I the yielding clay." That is the first step in the way to usefulness.

Picking up that lump of clay, he put it on the wheel, and with gentle but direct pressure in the right spots it began to take shape: a teapot with a perfectly fitting lid, a sugar basin and a cream jug, all set out on the board. Three useful things and yet all a part of a whole. The potter had these things in mind as he turned the wheel, and as he worked, he met with no resistance. That piece of clay was willing to be just a teapot, sugar basin and cream jug! The Lord, your Master Potter, has a purpose for you. Are you seeking great things for yourself? Seek them not, just lie still and let Him do the moulding as He chooses.

Then those vessels have to be dried and baked in a very hot oven for some time. As I glanced into the oven as we passed, I thought, Yes, that accounts for the testings we meet with. We need them if we are to be worthy and useful vessels. Without the baking they would be no use!

Then he took us into another room where some girls were very busy painting different designs on pottery already baked. The colours looked dull, blue, green, brown and yellow, but the master explained that, when they had been put in the oven again and re-baked and glazed, the colours would be vivid. Heat and more heat was necessary for a perfect piece of pottery!

I sauntered through the shop and looked at the many lovely things on the shelves, each so distinctive and with brilliant colouring. They managed to catch my eye, and I thought of all that those lumps of clay had been through to reach such perfection. Some were for a special use, and others just seemed to be lovely enough to adorn a home, but each was made according to the mind of the master. Vessels unto honour because from first to last it was yielded clay.

In Jeremiah 18:4 we find these words, "The vessel that he made of clay was marred in the hands of the potter: so he made it again another vessel, as it seemed good to the potter to make." He made it again! What comfort and hope that brings to the woman who takes a good look at her life and has to confess that it has been marred through some unwillingness to yield to God's pattern. You felt, didn't you, that you had better plans and did not want to go the way the Lord was pointing. You did not want to be just a teapot or cream jug as it were. You thought that you were capable of greater things; and now with a sad heart you realize what you have missed.

Dear friend, take heart again today as you read that verse, and remember that although the Lord was speaking of a nation, yet He deals with us as individuals in the same way. He knows the longing of your soul, and if you will deliberately yield to Him, He will make of you another vessel that will honour Him. Under the touch of the Master Potter that life of yours can be made one of beauty and usefulness.

Well, I hope that sharing with you our visit to the potter's house will have brought you a blessing, just as it did to me. A heart-searching prayer for us today would be:

> Have thine own way, Lord,
> Have thine own way,
> Thou art the Potter,
> I am the clay,
> Mould me and make me after thy will,
> While I am waiting,
> Yielded and still.

God bless you and answer your prayer.

## THE SHUNAMMITE (I)

> ". . . where was a great woman . . ."
> *2 Kings 4: 8*

WE are going to turn to 2 Kings 4 and share something about another woman. She was evidently a very practical woman, and her story reminded me of one I heard my pastor at home tell many years ago, of a very poor woman who always managed to have a cup of tea and something to eat for the friends who came to visit with her. Many people found their way to her home just because of the blessing they received from being with her because she was such a radiant Christian. Often they wondered how she managed to have things in the house. One day someone plucked up courage enough to ask her how she did it. With a smile she answered, "Oh,

that is easy, you see I just shovel out and the Lord shovels in."
No wonder she was rich in God and friends!

Well, let's look at the Shunammite woman. In verse 8 we read,
"It fell on a day, that Elisha [the prophet] passed to Shunem, where
was a great woman; and she constrained him to eat bread. And so it
was, that as oft as he passed by, he turned in thither to eat bread."

This much we know about her . . . that she was renowned.
People knew her and recognized her as a great woman. There
must have been something about her character that made her stand
out above others, and thus win for her this title. She was a woman
with spiritual perception, for she recognized Elisha as a man of God.
I think she must have been renowned, too, because she had a heart
big enough to take in others and look after their needs. The law of
kindness was something with which she was familiar.

But she was also realistic in her approach to life, and she faced the
fact that the prophet not only needed food to keep him going but
also a place to rest in. Now come some words that tell us more
about her. In verse 9, "She said to her husband, Behold now, I
perceive that this is an holy man of God, which passeth by us con-
tinually. Let us make a little chamber, I pray thee, on the wall; and
let us set for him there a bed, and a table, and a stool, and a candle-
stick: and it shall be, when he cometh to us, he shall turn in thither."

She said to her husband! She shared her convictions with him
and said, "Let us make". It is a blessed thing when wives can talk to
their husbands about the things that concern them, and they are of
one mind in what they do. Even though she was known as a great
woman, she acted in a spirit of oneness with her husband. There
was no selfishness about her. We often glibly speak of "A Prophet's
Chamber", but do we ever stop to think how it originated? Her
concern was for God's man, and she faced it realistically. "Let's
spend the money," she said, "on simple furnishings and necessary
things so that Elisha can have a place to rest when he comes here."
She verily was laying up treasure in heaven.

She was renowned, realistic, but she was also rewarded. A very
grateful prophet thanked her for all her thought. He did not walk
away and take it all for granted. No, he wanted to do something in
return. "What can we do for you?" he asked. "Speak to the king
on your behalf?" But she was content to dwell among her own

people and serve as opportunity arose. However, Elisha, who had received only good at her hands, did not leave it there. Her reward came in the gift of a son that she had so much desired.

Does this record spark off a chord in your own heart? It is wonderful for a woman to be known because of her thought and kindness for others, and we don't need to be rich in this world's goods to have a share in helping another. There are needy people all around us. There are many of God's children who are looking for such a woman. Maybe there is just some way you could help another and be the channel that God would use to supply her need. Is He talking to your heart at this very moment about someone? Has some name flashed upon your mind? Is there something you could do to relieve that one? Maybe you hesitate as you look upon the meagreness of your own supply, but if God is prompting you to do it, don't be afraid, for just as fast as you give out, God will give to you.

Opportunities of serving the Lord come to us all in different ways. God is no man's debtor. He always gives the Much More. How many people miss the richness of fellowship with some of God's choicest servants because they have a closed heart and a closed home. You remember that Lydia in the Book of Acts was one of those women whose heart the Lord opened, and she in turn opened her home and put it at His disposal.

This is essentially a woman's job. I know so well a certain home in the north of Ireland that was always open to the Lord's people through the most stringent times of war. Somehow, however many people came, there was always enough to feed them. The Lord saw to that! Sometimes someone would slip in with an extra packet of margarine or a ration of sugar that they could ill afford to part with! What blessing resulted far and wide through that open home, and how many grateful hearts crossed the threshold of that door. God gives to us a precious ministry in our homes, so let's make use of it and reap the blessing.

Renowned, realistic and rewarded.

"God is not unrighteous to forget your work and labour of love." *Hebrews 6: 10*

THE story of the Shunammite woman last time set me thinking of the words of a once familiar hymn which says:

Have you on the Lord believed? still there's more to follow.
Have you of His grace received? still there's more to follow.

Surely there was an experience of the "much more" that God gives when we seek Him.

You remember that we saw her as a renowned woman, one who faced the problems and needs of others realistically, and consequently she was rewarded by God with the gift of a son. The Lord will be debtor to no man, and there is a verse in Hebrews 6 which reads, "God is not unrighteous to forget your work and labour of love, which ye have showed toward his name, in that ye ministered to the saints, and do minister." God will not forget even if everyone else does! But let's go back to 2 Kings 4 and see how God worked and provided for this particular woman. Because with all her greatness, she was subject to the everyday trials of life just as we are.

She suddenly finds herself walking the path of sorrow. What was her God-given reward seems to have been so soon snatched from her in the death of the loved son. She would surely wonder why this had happened, and bewilderment would fill her soul in this hour of grief. Yet, even now her thoughts turn again to the prophet Elisha whom she had recognized as a man of God, and hope springs up in her heart as she puts her boy down on the bed Elisha had used. With hope in one hand and desperation in the other, she goes out to look for the prophet. Nothing and no one is allowed to stand in her way.

Eventually she finds him and pours out her story. Once again he has time to listen to her and sends his servant to the home to act for

him, but she will have none of that. Elisha, the man she knows to
be God's man, must come himself! The servant Gehazi proves the
fact that the child is dead, but see Elisha as he enters the room that
was familiar to him. He prays. He realizes that apart from God he
can do nothing, but as he prays he draws from the hand of God that
which he needs in this hour of crisis. Then stretching himself upon
the child, identifies himself with him and life returns.

When a baby is born, a nurse is always glad to hear that first cry,
for it tells her so much that is vital. Here this child sneezes and
opens his eyes, and he is handed back to his mother. Sorrow is
turned into joy as she takes her child in her arms. Hers is a continuing reward. But the end is not yet. Still there is more to follow!
We read of God's wonderful care for her and His provision for her
daily need!

There is an impending famine in the land, and she is singled out
and warned to go to another place where she will find food for her
family. Taking the advice of the prophet, she goes to the land of the
Philistines and lives there for seven years. Then she decides it is time
to go back home again. But what will she find when she gets there?
Things will not be as she had left them.

She goes to the king to plead for a return of her home and lands.
It so happened that when she got there Elisha's servant was there,
and at that moment the king was actually asking him about the
wonderful things that Elisha had been doing. They were talking of
the raising of her son to life, and as Gehazi looks around there she is
right there! He says, "Let her tell the story in her own words!" The
king was so impressed that he gave an order for the complete restor-
ation of all that was hers! This wonderful glimpse into the life of
this woman speaks for itself, but let us just look at ourselves for a
minute in the light of it.

When you tread a pathway of sorrow, to whom do you turn for
help and succour? She had to go in search of Elisha and that meant
time and energy. But you have One with you so near who has time
to listen to your story as you pour it out to Him. He will not turn
you away or send you to someone else for comfort. Many of our so-
called friends have ceased to have a heart at leisure to soothe and
sympathize with the needs of others, but in Jesus you have a never-
failing friend whose Presence is always with you.

Did you notice the expression that I used, "It so happened"? But did it? God was in the life of this woman, and He was concerned for her. His care would never end, and He brought about the various circumstances that were used to restore to her the property and lands that had once been hers.

God is always on time. He can order everything for you, your steps and your stops. And He can cause all things to work together for good to them that love Him. Do you watch for the hand of God in the daily events in your life? How He can just weave things together! He even moved the heart of the king on her behalf, and there is no end to what God will do for us if we will only trust Him.

Are you treading a difficult path as you care for the needs of others? Does it sometimes seem a thankless task? Then take heart. God is not unrighteous to forget. He takes note of it all and His reward will be worth having.

Just for today as we go about our different duties, let's sum it up in a way that will help us through. God's care for you will never cease. His provision will never fail you, and His Presence will never leave you. What more can we ask?

## THE ETERNAL HOME

> "Here we have no continuing city, but we seek one to come." *Hebrews 13:14*

THOUGHTS of home reminded me the other day of that lovely old hymn we don't hear much these days, but which has lifted and cheered the heart of many a Christian through the years, and still will, I am sure, wherever it is sung:

> The dear old story of a Saviour's love,
> Is sweeter as the days go by,
> The glad assurance of a home above
> Is sweeter as the days go by.

Some of us had been talking together about the problems of moving house. You know what that involves, for, no matter how careful you are, things seem to have a way of collecting and it just seems too much to think of starting to pack! One of our group was telling us how they found things made comparatively easy for them because the removers just took everything into their hands and told them not to worry. They would deposit everything as it was and where they wanted it. Not even their clothes or china had to be packed! That was something worth knowing.

Then my mind went on a bit further as I thought of all the people one hears about who are constantly on the move! No sooner does the furniture van arrive with their goods than it seems to be there again taking them somewhere else! There are people like that who are "here today and gone tomorrow" sort of thing. They live in tumult of packing and, as they say in Ireland, "flitting!" No fixed abode, no roots going down!

All of this led me on to the verse in the Bible which says of us Christians, "Here have we no continuing city, but we seek one to come." A place where we won't always be on the move! Such a blessed thought takes us right out of this world of change and into the land that is fairer than day, where Eternal Love has provided a dwelling place for us. As the Psalmist said, "I will dwell in the house of the Lord for ever." No change, no decay there!

There are people, of course, who for different reasons find themselves having to give up the home they have loved for many years. Maybe you are one of them! You have become so attached to it. Your cherished possessions. Every room stored with precious memories. Your garden, your friendly neighbours and even the shopkeepers with whom you dealt. It is all part of you, and the thought of having to yield to it almost knocks you down. You feel you just can't bear to begin all over again. Sorrow fills your heart and oppresses your mind as you contemplate all that is involved. How often you say to yourself that no other place on earth could be quite like this one!

Dear friend, I want to bring to you a word of comfort and cheer. Just for these few moments look up into the face of your Saviour who is saying to you, "I go to prepare a place for you." Surely, He knows all about the strain of your uprooting, your distress and your longings. But He has you in mind, and up there in the Glory He is preparing a place for you. It will be a place from which you can never be evicted and never have to leave. No one can take it from you, and I know you will be fully satisfied with what His great love provides for you!

Yes, when change takes place down here and fetters begin to break, let the glad assurance of a home above fill your heart and chase away the gloom! However wonderful your home down here, it cannot compare with that in the City Bright! There is a wonderful prospect in front of you.

This brings to mind just now an experience of mine when I was but a child, but which has lived with me through the years. As a family, we were leaving England to go over to Ireland, and that meant all the usual bustle of packing and good-byes and excitement for us children. How well I recall getting into the taxi in Aldershot and a friend pressing a sixpence into my hand. I thought that was the highest reward possible! We travelled on by train and eventually boarded the boat. It was a terrible night. The winds raged and that ship tossed and pitched, and, of course, we were frightened. I kept saying to my mother, "I want to go home. I don't like this." "I want to go home" was my refrain and it must have disturbed her greatly.

A friend who was travelling with us put her arm around me and, thinking she was comforting me, said, "But, Norah, out here on this rough sea, you have no home to go to." No home to go to! It was depressing and worrying to a child, to say the least. But when we finally arrived at our destination and friends greeted us and with outstretched arms took us in to their homes, the night lost its terror! We were safe at home!

No home to go to! Is it possible that there happens to be someone reading today, and you know that if you had to leave your home of this world today, you have no heavenly home to go to. Are you so attached to the things of earth that you have not given a thought to what will happen to you throughout Eternity? It is a long time to be without a home. There is a Saviour who stands waiting to receive you if you will only come to Him. He will deal with the sin that separates you from Him and prepare you for the Home in Heaven that He has gone to prepare for you. You just don't know when your time will come, so do not delay trusting Him, but make Him yours today. Share with me, too, the glad assurance of a home above.

The Lord will take care of the future for you and me. I know He is preparing something wonderful for us, so if your heart has been downcast at your seeming losses, just take a look at what the future holds, through His Eternal Love. Enjoy your home while you have it and make it a happy place for all who enter, but set your lasting affections on things above. God bless you.

## SHORT CUTS!

"I am the Way. . . ." *John 14:6*

WHENEVER I see a bull or a cow I am reminded of an incident when my sister and I were having a holiday up in the country for the first time away from home. To the town dweller there are all sorts of fascinating things, even going out to gather the eggs was a great delight, for it was something new. Helping to feed the animals and taking tea down to the men who were working in the fields, it was all fun and real holiday to us. But, oh dear, and it was a big BUT, there were those cows with their big horns and large eyes. I was always sure that they were coming straight for us. Over the little bridge that was near by my sister and I would jump until they were safely out of our way. How our cousins laughed at us, but prevention was better than cure in my eyes! I never did lose my fear of what they called gentle cows! Just how could they be!

On one occasion two of us were visiting in another home and had to get back to my aunt with whom we were staying. These friends pointed out the fields that lay between us and suggested that we jump over the stiles, cross the fields, and the house we could see on the top of the hill was ours. We thought this was great to take a short cut, and started off bravely enough, and had just climbed with laughter the last stile and taken a few steps through the grass when we heard an awful noise not far away. One look, and terror gave wings to our feet and screams as well. We hardly knew where we were running, but there was that bull, puffing for all he was

B

worth, coming after us with his head down. Our cries brought my aunt to the door and soon she was there beside us shouting instructions while she got between us and the bull with a huge stick. Scratched and sore, we worked our way through the thorn hedge and she after us. We turned to see that steaming bull facing us on the other side.

When we had time to recover and were going the last steps through the meadow that led to home, Auntie said, "What made them tell you to take the short cut? They know there is always a bull there."

Over and over again that day has lived to me when I have thought about taking short cuts. There is no safe short cut when it comes to following the Lord. So often we look for them, only to find them full of dangers. Yes, we were going home, but the short cut proved the wrong way. The same applies to our Eternal Home. There is no short cut, and if there is someone who thinks that she knows better and can reach the Heavenly Home other than by the way God has made for us, you are doomed to eternal disappointment unless you come His way. Lots of folk are out to try and take short cuts to get to Heaven, for it has a wonderful attraction, and in their hearts they want to know that they will be there some day, but they don't want to come God's way. Does that apply to you today? If so, listen:

> I must needs go home by the way of the Cross,
> There is no other way but this,
> I shall ne'er get sight of the gates of light,
> If the way of the Cross I miss.

Don't try to get to Heaven your own way, for it is fraught with disaster and will only lead you at last to despair and separation from God. You can add up all sorts of things that seem good to you, but they are shifting sands upon which you will perish. The Bible tells us that "There is a way that seemeth right unto man, but the end thereof are the ways of death."

In John 14:6 the Lord was talking to His troubled disciples about where He was going to prepare a place for them and He said, "I am the way, the truth and the life: no man cometh unto the Father, but by me." No other way and no other name! All your good intentions, ideas and ambitions are short cuts and will never open to you the door into the Eternal Home in Heaven. You must needs enter by the way of the Cross, for it was on that Cross the Lord Jesus became sin for you that He might bring you to God.

Christian friend, with the great hope of Heaven in your heart, do you ever find yourself wanting to take short cuts to blessing and find that they don't pay? I often think about this when I am busy in my kitchen. Time is limited, and somehow the clock seems to tick so quickly. That cake in the oven just must be done by a certain time. The temptation comes to turn up the gas just a wee bit higher, but, oh dear, the minute you take the cake out of the oven, down it goes. It was not given time enough at the right temperature!

Just so, don't try to take short cuts in your spiritual life. Give yourself time. Give God time to work out the pattern He has in mind for you, and don't forget that His plan for you will not be the same as that for your sister.

I think I read somewhere once the words "Your impatience measured against His perfect knowledge." How far short we come because of our impatience to get on and see things done. God is not in a hurry. His clock is never fast or slow, but always on time. If you are prepared to go His way, wait His time, the blessing will come, and all blessing comes to us by the way of the Cross.

> I must needs go on in the Blood sprinkled way,
> The path that the Saviour trod.
> If I ever climb to the heights sublime,
> Where the soul is at home with God.

See that child stamping her feet with impatience to get her way. Exasperation gets into her voice, but the mother who knows best quietly says, "We are not ready yet." The Lord often has to say that to us, so listen to Him and don't take short cuts, let Him lead you on step by step along the road that leads Home. For you will find:

> It is sweet to know as you onward go,
> That the way of the Cross leads home.

## FORGIVENESS

WHEN I was busy about the house the other day, I was suddenly conscious that I was humming a hymn I had not heard for some time. The last line of the chorus kept coming back to me. Then I recalled the four lines, which were:

> He the pearly gates will open
> So that I may enter in,
> For he purchased my redemption,
> And forgave me all my sin.

It came to mind as we had been reading together Psalm 32. David's expression of "forgiveness" had in a special way caught my attention. Anyway, as I tidied up I kept going over the words, "He forgave me all my sin", and realized it was a wonderful note for the rest of the day.

In the middle of the morning I remembered a story I had read of a little lad who had done some wrong. He was not aware of the seriousness of it, but his elders were greatly disturbed by it and felt that he should be made to feel it too! The time came when he found himself in a room with them all. There they sat as stern as a row of judges about to pass sentence. Not a flicker of a smile for the wee fellow. With tear-stained face he looked up at his loved nurse, but, oh dear, she was as stern as the rest of them. He scanned their faces one by one, but there was not the slightest sign of relenting on any one of them. It was awful, and hurt so badly. Finally, with a sob in his voice and the tears wet on his cheeks, he looked up from the floor and said, "Oh, won't somebody forgive me?" The greatest longing of his heart was to know and feel that he was forgiven. But how cold human hearts can sometimes be!

Yes, David was talking about "forgiveness" and tells us how he came to experience it for himself. He had been fully aware of his sin. It was like a weight by day and night, but in verse 5 he says, "I acknowledged my sin unto Thee . . . and Thou forgavest."

There was no excusing or hiding of his sin. It was by way of confession and repentance that he came to taste the sweetness of God's forgiveness, and that, of course, is just where real life begins for each of us when we come to Jesus as a sinner. Oh, I do hope that its message is music in your ears today, and that the sense of His forgiveness will bring cheer and uplift into your heart that will radiate to those with whom you will be in contact through the hours of the day. Be like David, tell somebody about it! "Blessed is the one whose transgression is forgiven, whose sin is covered." Blotted out, never to be remembered. Covered by the precious blood of the Saviour, never to be uncovered! The grace and the mercy of God should fill our hearts with singing.

We can look to a wonderful future because we have been forgiven. As the hymn says:

> He the pearly gates will open
> So that I may enter in.

That is linking past and future together. What about the present day in which we have to live and face up to realities? David, what about that? Look at verse 6. Forgiveness leads the way and opens up to a door into a fuller experience of the love and care of our Heavenly Father. We have acceptance and assurance, but also a door of access to the Lord Himself at all times.

Let us read what he says: "For this, shall every one that is godly pray unto Thee in a time when Thou mayest be found: surely in the floods of great waters they shall not come nigh unto him." An open door to God through prayer in every time of need! Making your requests known to Him, AND HE WILL BE FOUND! His ears open to your cry, and His eyes upon you for good! Troubles may find their way into the threads of your life. The waters of sorrow or affliction may creep up to your door, but they will not overwhelm. Don't ever forget that the measuring cup is in the hands of the Lord who loves you and knows when to stay it! He will be always alert to your need. The longings and prayers of the one He has forgiven will be His concern. You have the right of access to Him to plead your cause, whatever it be at this moment.

But then David goes even a step further! The door is not just ajar, but widely open, welcoming you and me to enter and enjoy the things that God has prepared for us. "Thou art my hiding place." He was very familiar with the need for a place to hide in, particularly when his enemies chased him from one spot to another, but he knew too the need for a hiding place from the taunts and scorn that were heaped upon him.

He found the Lord to be his hiding place, his refuge, and so may you when the enemy would hurl his fiery darts at you. I know of a certainty that you won't be long without them once you belong to the Lord. They will come at you from all kinds of places that you never expected, but you have a hiding place. A place of Safety, a place of Refuge, because the Lord is your Refuge. You can run to Him and be safe. Hidden in Christ. Not speculation but reality!

David knew the battles of daily life. He faced up to the pressures and anxieties, but let us listen to him just once more today. "Thou shalt preserve me from trouble; Thou shalt compass me about with songs of deliverance." All of this because he has his feet on the right road and began at the right place. Forgiveness. Be the way ever so hard, there are songs of deliverance for the trusting child of God. He will prepare deliverance for you that will cause you to sing! Just when things might seem at their darkest, He will give you a song! He will be the author of it! He will make you glad through the works of His hands.

## EMERGENCIES

"Lord, save me." *Matthew 14:30*

IT was just one of those days again, when I was busy about the ordinary tasks of every day, sweeping floors, making beds, dusting and cooking, when I was startled to hear the clanging bell as the fire engine rushed past, then the shrill whistle of the police car, and the imperative demand of the ambulance to get first place among the traffic. Where could they be going? I wondered. It was an emergency call. As I went about my work thinking about emergencies, and all the unexpected things that can arise before the day is over, I remembered that somewhere I had seen the words written "emergency prayers". I began to think of some of the times when I had lifted up my heart to God with just a few words or even an unspoken petition in a particular time of need, and found an answer. Those were emergencies to me, when I needed help.

You can find this type of prayer all through the Bible, born out of a deep heart longing, a cry for help in a desperate position. A look up for wisdom in a moment of need, and always the Lord was at hand to answer.

There was Nehemiah, for instance, a man with a burden on his heart. He stood before the king, carrying out his routine duties, but his trouble was expressed in his sad countenance. "What is wrong?" asked the king. "What is it you want?" And just as quickly Nehemiah shot up a prayer to the God of Heaven for wisdom. Being directed, he told his story to the king, and, however impossible it had seemed to him before, his request was granted. Nehemiah in that moment had dealings with the King of Kings, and He moved the heart of the earthly king.

As a Christian, do you ever find yourself in a tight corner and you don't know what your very next words should be? Well, if you are walking in fellowship with the Lord, why not do as Nehemiah, and in a moment of time with or without words look to the Lord for what you should do or how you should answer. He has promised to be wisdom to you. An upward look and His Spirit will guide you just at the right moment.

Just think of how many times David uttered those heart cries to God and was heard. The suddenness of events made him turn often to the Lord, not with flowery language, but the simple expressions of deep need, and he was heard. The same thing can be said of so many of God's people.

There are some short prayers of people in the New Testament that touch our lives, too. I was reading again of the prayer that was uttered by the thief when he hung on the cross. He was conscious of the fact that he was thus suffering because of his own crimes, but that punishment did not take away the sense of his guilt before God. In the very Presence of the Lord Jesus Christ on the cross beside him he recognized the Holy One of God, the Saviour, and with all the passion of his heart in that late hour, as he faced eternity, his only plea was, "Lord, remember me." It was indeed at once the acknowledgement of his need and his faith in the power of Christ to save him. He had gone his own way, but now as eternity stares him in the face he is well aware of the fact that he needs someone to stand between him and God, a Redeemer, and he found Him in the Saviour who heard his cry and gave the ready answer, "Today shalt thou be with me in Paradise." When such a prayer is wrung from any heart, there will always be an answer of assurance from the Lord.

> The dying thief rejoiced to see that fountain in his day,
> And there have I though vile as he washed all my sin away.

Have you ever prayed that kind of prayer? It is the only kind that will ever give you the right to expect God to hear and answer you in other emergencies of life. So many people, when a crisis comes, expect God to hear their so-called prayers, but only the one who has first trusted Him as Saviour can expect answers. If you know Him, you can with confidence call upon Him at all times.

I often think of Peter in this respect. That episode in Matthew 14 shows him in a real dilemma due to a lack of faith on his part, something most of us have experienced at one time or another. With others he was in the boat when the storm arose. The waves tossed them to and fro. They thought they were alone on that stretch of water. They had left Jesus with the crowd, but right there in the midst of the tempest He comes walking on the water towards them. He had a concern for them, and He has for you, too, in the tempest of life. "It is I," He said, stilling their fears, but there is Peter who wants further confirmation. He said, "Lord, if it be Thou, bid me come unto Thee on the water." Getting the invitation, "Come," he sets out to walk on the water to Jesus. All went well until the waves loomed far bigger than the Lord who called him. That was where he began to sink, but in that moment of desperate need and emergency in his life, he cried out, "Lord, save me." At once he found the comforting powerful hand of the Lord gripping him and rescuing.

It was a simple prayer, but there was desperation in it. Do you ever find yourself sinking, succumbing to the circumstances that surround you, simply because you have taken your eyes off the Lord who called you? It is so human to look at the things that appear so immense and lose sight of the Presence of the Lord who is always at hand, and yet, He wants to show you through these very things that He is greater far than the turbulence and storms of life. He wants to let you know that He is always at hand.

Have the buffetings and trials that come your way so taken hold of you that you are beginning to sink? Faith is dimmed, discouragement has taken hold of you, but you long to reach out to Him again. Dear friend, be assured that His hand is always stretched out to save. If, like Peter, your prayer is short but from the depths of your heart, you will find He will take your hand and uphold you. It is so good to know that, in all the distresses and emergencies of life, the Christian woman can reach out and find the help she needs. Let your emergencies lead you to Christ.

## A BROKEN CONFIDENCE

> "It is better to trust in the Lord than to put
> confidence in man." *Psalm 118: 8*

THE other day I was recalling the time when I visited a friend whom I am going to call Mrs. Green. I knocked on her door, and, after waiting some time, I was just about ready to go away when the door opened. One glance showed her tear-stained face and red eyes. I wondered right away what could have happened.

She pointed me to her living-room, and as we sat down grief overcame her again, and down went her head as the tears overflowed! Without knowing what was the cause of it all, I tried to comfort her. Then I felt that maybe it was best to let the tears flow, so I slipped away to her kitchen and put on the kettle and made a cup of tea. You see, I had been in her kitchen before so knew where to get things! She looked up at the rattle of the cups when I entered the room again with the tray. I encouraged her to have a cup! Eventually she was calm enough to tell me a bit about what was troubling her.

She had a friend, let us call her Miss Brown, who often visited her. One day as they sat alone she confided to her a very great trouble she had known, believing that she could trust her implicitly with it. She had kept it locked up in her heart for so long that finally she felt she must tell someone. The telling of it brought her a measure of relief.

Then later, to her dismay, she discovered that Miss Brown had left and gone to visit with another woman. As they sat gossiping together about this and that, something came up about Mrs. Green. Miss Brown, anxious to make an impression, let this other person know that she was in Mrs. Green's confidence. She said she knew something about her that no one else knew of. She leaned a bit closer and said, "Between you and me and the gate-post, Mrs. Green told me . . ." and before long the whole story was out into the ears of another. The confidence with which she was entrusted was shattered. The tragic thing was that it did not end there, for the whisper was passed from one to the other until it went in a complete circle and found its way back to Mrs. Green. No wonder she was in tears that day!

It was hard for her now to face people because she was aware that many knew the secret she had carried quietly for so long. She was conscious all the time of their looks as she passed by and the whispers! It was a very real experience, and not for anything would I have been in the shoes of Miss Brown. I had often heard her say to others, "Between you and me and the gate-post," and it always seemed to me that she had far too many gate-posts on her lists! So here she was, the cause of a broken confidence and intense suffering. Who can bear that sort of let-down? Certainly here Mrs. Green would never go to her again in a time of need. If you have ever tasted the same sort of thing you will have all the sympathy in the world with Mrs. Green.

In Proverbs 25:19 we read, "Confidence in an unfaithful man [or woman, of course] in time of trouble is like a broken tooth, and a foot out of joint", and that spells suffering. As Mrs. Green and I talked together, we found that the Scriptures are full of warnings along this line, so no wonder we read in the Psalms that it is better to "trust in the Lord than put confidence in man". I am well aware that there are times when the Lord gives to us a friend who will stand by us in an hour of deep need, knowing that, when she says she will be as "silent as the grave" about it, she means it and keeps her word.

Together we talked about such times and were able to thank God for such faithful friends. We put thoughts of Miss Brown aside for a few moments while we reflected on one precious thought that in our Saviour we can place all our confidence and know it is safe with Him. We can talk to Him about everything that concerns us. Our very deepest needs and heart longings included. We can confide in Him about the reason for every sorrow we bear. We can tell Him our every thought and know with assurance that He will never let us down.

> What a friend we have in Jesus,
>   All our sins and griefs to bear!
> What a privilege to carry
>   Everything to God in prayer.

Did you know, Mrs. Green, that the author of that hymn was an Irishman whose fiancée was drowned on the eve of their wedding? He had known suffering and proved the Lord as his friend.

Let us read another verse that has been a great help to me in times of stress and strain. Proverbs 3:26, "The Lord shall be thy confidence, and shall keep thy foot from being taken." Yes, He is there to stand by and support you. Just now in this particular thing that you are going through, you can make Him your Confidant, and how well you can trust Him with every secret you have and even with those who have harmed you. The wonderful thing about making the Lord your Confidant is that you need never have a lurking dread or fear that what you have told Him will ever leak out! You can have His listening ear for the things you cannot share with another and have the love of His understanding heart.

Maybe you have felt the sorrow of being let down by your particular Miss Brown—one who proved herself unworthy of your trust. I am sure the Lord has much to say to her if only she will listen. But so far as you are concerned today, open your heart and tell the Lord in words all about it and leave it with Him. He will be the drier of your tears and the lifter up of your head. Oh, yes, He will safeguard that which you commit to Him.

> There's no other friend so keen to help you
> No other friend so quick to hear,
> No other place to leave your burden,
> No other one to hear your prayer.
> So all your anxiety, all your care,
> Bring to the mercy seat, leave it there.

And the Lord be your special Confidant today.


## HONOURING GOD

"Them that honour me I will honour."
*I Samuel 2: 30*

ONE day my husband and I were having lunch with some visiting friends. After we had given thanks to the Lord for His provision for us, one of our number said, "I must tell you of something interesting that happened to a Christian acquaintance of ours."

The man was away from home on business, so he went into a restaurant for a meal. He found a table, sat down, looked at the menu and decided what he would have. While he was waiting to be served, he bowed his head and said Grace. His meal was brought and he enjoyed it. Then it was time to be on his way again. He reached into his pocket for his wallet to pay the bill. Then he remembered that he had changed his suit and had forgotten to transfer it. His wallet was at home! "What shall I do?" he thought.

He went to the cash desk to leave his name and address on a slip of paper and promise to come in and pay next day. When it was almost his turn, he felt a hand on his shoulder. A voice said, "Step over here a minute." It was the manager. What could he want? "This morning," he said, "I promised the Lord that I would give a free meal to the first person I saw bowing his head to ask a blessing. No need for you to pay your bill. You are that person!" You can imagine his feelings, can't you?

This actually happened in England, and as I listened to the story in Monte Carlo, there flashed into my mind the words from I Samuel 2: 30, "Them that honour me I will honour." It was such a simple thing in the everyday life of a Christian, but other eyes were watching for someone who shared a like faith and was not ashamed of it. The eyes of the Lord were upon him, too!

That lunch-hour reminded me again of God's faithfulness. As I read those words in context, "Them that honour me I will honour", they stood out both as a rebuke and a challenge. Give to God what belongs to Him, and He will take care of all things for you. Oh, yes, those wicked sons of Eli not only gave way to vice and sin but they deliberately chose to rob God and misuse the things that belonged to Him. The Lord had to speak plainly to them and tell them that they had forfeited His promised blessing.

Write it upon your heart today, "Them that honour me I will honour." They are words that can burn themselves into our hearts with either conviction or blessing. They can be a guide when we are faced with some particular question in our lives.

Looking over the lives of many of the Biblical characters, we see how God fulfilled this very word to them as they sought to honour Him under all kinds of stress and strain. There was Joseph. Just take a look at his experience! Cast out, sold, unjustly accused, imprisoned, forgotten, yes, by all; but God, whose watchful eyes were upon him, brought him through every valley of testing and eventually raised him to an honoured position. God will never be too late, and it is good to be in His honours list.

There was Moses. If ever a man had a chance to win worldly fame and gains for himself, it was surely he. Life in a palace with all its privileges, plus, of course, its sins and its pleasures, but he deliberately chose to refuse the lesser, and honour God. You know how He made him to be a leader of His people! He was faced with a hard task, an unenviable one, almost every step of the way, but in honouring God, facing life's responsibilities, he was honoured!

What about it in our own homes? Do we take our stand even when others do not share our faith? Do we honour God by our quiet actions and let Him take care of the results?

There was Samuel: one so very young, but who put God first, and sought to exalt Him. God honoured him. There was Daniel, faced with problems of all kinds and the making of decisions that would show where he stood in relation to the Lord. He determined to live a God-honouring life before all classes and kinds of people.

He purposed in his heart, and God gave him favour and used him. And so it goes on right through the Bible. Just as a closing thought, let's look at one whose name was Mary.

When you have time, turn to Mark 14 and read verses 3-9. She had in her possession something very precious. It was costly, and something that she would normally have hugged to herself, just because of its very value. One day she takes a look at it. While she holds it in her hands, she makes up her mind. Only the very best is fit for the One who has done so much for her. Him she would honour with what she possessed. So she goes with the box of precious ointment in her hand. As she comes near to the Lord, she breaks it and anoints Him with the fragrant contents!

All at once there was a change in the atmosphere. Fragrance filled the air, but on the other hand there were those who raised their voices in protest! Surely this was not necessary. Sheer waste! But listen to the Lord. "Let her alone; . . . she hath wrought a good work on me. . . . Wheresoever this Gospel shall be preached throughout the whole world, this also that she hath done shall be spoken of for a memorial of her."

That is why you and I are reading it today! She honoured Him in giving her most precious thing, and He saw to it that she was honoured for all time! Mary, just an ordinary woman, a sinner, saved by grace. Let others accuse her if they would, her heart responded in worship to Him, and she could safely leave her critics to Him. So can you!

Don't you find yourself sometimes asking, shall I do this or that! Will I use this for myself or give it to the Lord? Never be ashamed to own Him in word or deed. Put Him to the test and remember even for today "Them that honour me I will honour". Make your decisions in favour of Him whose eyes are upon you.

# KNITTING

*"What is that in thine hand?"* Exodus
4: 2

PERHAPS you are one of those many women I have seen travelling
by bus and train who carry their knitting with them everywhere
they go and utilize the moments adding on the rows! It gives a
feeling of satisfaction, and to the onlooker it is fascinating to watch
the needles moving at full speed. Even in the doctor's waiting-room
you will sometimes find a knitter. I was a great knitter myself once
upon a time. I think I have made about everything from a baby's
bootee, or a doll's, for that matter, to a dress. Pullovers and cardi-
gans and all the rest, and many a thing I learned as the needles
clicked to and fro!

When I was a missionary, I started a knitting class for girls. They
eventually learned to knit simple stitches, with increases and
decreases and so on, and while they were doing it, they were teaching me something in the school of patience.

Does the Bible have anything to say to us knitters? In a sense, no,
yet it can stir up our thoughts as we work and set them upon the
Lord. Let us see what we can find for our good. You are all
familiar with the words, "Cast on", and that means there must
always be a beginning. Not much use having the needles and wool
in your hands, and even the pattern before you, if you don't start
casting on. You must begin by using the things already in your
hand. This reminds me of a verse in Exodus 4, where the Lord asked
of Moses, "What is that in thine hand?" Just a rod! But see what
use God made of the thing in his hand!

Take a good look and see if God has entrusted you with some
gift that He wants you to begin using. Casting on stitches, as it
were, the very beginning of a piece of work for Him. Oh, it could
even be your knowledge of knitting that could be used to help
another who is not so capable in that respect as you are. In so many
simple everyday ways you can begin to do things you never thought

of. Cast on one stitch at a time, and soon the needles will carry the increasing weight of your work.

That thought takes me right over to a very precious verse in 1 Peter 5:7, one you know so well, but one I would suggest you think about when you are knitting. It won't surprise me if your job becomes one of relaxation when the Lord is in your thoughts. Listen, "Casting all your care upon Him, for He careth for you." You add an extra stitch at a time to your garment and the weight on your needles gets heavier, but the wool in your hand or lap gets lighter!

Why is it so hard to learn to cast on Him every care! So often we want to hold on to our troubles, and even caress them, instead of handing them over to the One who will bear all the weight, because He cares for you. I remember so well in that class there were girls who were content at first just to sit and look at the wool in their hands, until they woke up to the fact that someone else was making headway and enjoying it! Then there was no holding them back.

It is like that in our lives. Once we learn the secret of casting our care on the Lord deliberately, we want to go on doing it. Remember the wonderful invitation you have from the Lord in Psalm 55, "Cast thy burden on the Lord, and he shall sustain thee."

Then what about the pattern you have in your hand? You are just as anxious as I ever was to get it worked out perfectly, but you know to do that every instruction has to be followed. The correct size of needles, the right wool to give the proper tension. In every stitch you have to follow the instructions. You know the feeling of wanting so much to see how it is going to turn out, and you work feverishly to get through the first six or eight or ten rows of pattern just to satisfy yourself! Most of us are like that when we are attempting something new, but there is a good thought for us here.

The Lord has a pattern for your life and the word of God should be your guide in all things. "Thy word is a lamp unto my feet, and a light unto my path." It is only as you look to Him and follow His instructions that the pattern He had planned will be worked out. Once you take your eyes off Him and go the way you think best, it will be spoiled. Oh, the dropped stitches and ruined work I had to deal with in that class, because so often the girls would let their

that way when we deviate from God's appointed path for us. What bitter regrets it can work in us. Closing his mind to the claims of God on him, Jonah falls asleep, trying to assure himself that all was well.

But suddenly he gets a rude awakening! A great wind arose. Tempestuous seas, terrified mariners, all combine to shake him out of his false sense of security. He finds himself faced by the distressed and angry seamen. "Give an account of yourself," they demanded. "Who are you? What are you doing here? Where are you going?" Yes, he is beginning to realize that the path of disobedience is not worth the money exacted from him for his fare. It leads downhill and gets harder all the way. See, too, how he involved others and got them into a dangerous position. We never travel the downward path alone. What a tragic testimony from a man to whom God had committed a task He wanted him to do. Fleeing from the Presence of the Lord.

Maybe you thought there was nothing in the story of Jonah for you. It is just an Old Testament story that does not touch your life. Tell me, do you still think so? I think it might bring to life some experience of yours. It could be that the Lord has been talking to you about something He wants you to do for Him. Oh, not nearly such a difficult task as He gave to Jonah. But you have been making for yourself the proverbial one hundred and one excuses. There is a Nineveh somewhere in your life today, and you have been searching for a ship to get away from it. Anything rather than do what God is asking! Maybe He wants you to speak to just one person, perhaps your neighbour, not a whole city. And you dilly-dally, reluctant to obey His voice. It is your lips that He wants to make use of, but in that heart of yours you rebel and think someone else can do it.

How easy it is to wrap yourself around with all kinds of flimsy excuses. There is that letter He has been asking you to write, but you just won't take up your pen even to begin it. You feel that the other person has a right to act first! Like Jonah, you are paying the price of disobedience, and what a costly thing it is going to be in the end! Your peace has already been shattered, and the sweetness of God's presence is missing.

Is it some seemingly greater choice that you have to make? Even as you arose this morning, your mind was made up to go your own way, knowing that it is contrary to what the voice of God whispers to you. Dear Christian friend, heed the warning in today's chapter and turn with all your heart to do God's will, which will bring you lasting blessing and save you from the disasters that follow the path of disobedience.

We will come back to Jonah another time and follow God's ways with him, but take with you today the reminder that:

> The favour He shows, and the joy He bestows
> Are for them who will trust and obey.

What He asks of you He will enable you to do.


## JONAH REMORSEFUL

*"I will look again . . ." Jonah 2:4*

LET us go back to poor old Jonah. We left him in the boat being battered about by rough seas and angry seamen. These bewildered sailors fastened the blame for it all on him. There was no other apparent reason why such a storm should have blown up just then, and, of course, Jonah knew full well that there was no use denying it.

In chapter 1, verse 12 he frankly admits it, and that was something in his favour. "Take me up, and cast me forth into the sea," he says, "so shall the sea be calm unto you: for I know that for my sake this great tempest is upon you." In other words, "I am the cause of it all because of something I have done."

They were reluctant to throw him overboard, and tried hard to save the ship and themselves, but that sea was too angry for them. Finally, in sheer desperation, they tossed Jonah into the water. Immediately it ceased its raging and there was a calm. They were so thankful that they offered a sacrifice to the Lord. But out there in the deep was Jonah. They possibly thought that was the end of him, but, of course, God had other plans. What utter confusion his rebellion brought to him. Paying the fare to escape from God was not paying off. Of course, it never does!

Down into the sea; but the God whose voice he had disobeyed, the God of infinite love, mercy and patience, was looking after him. Even there in the very depths of the sea, as low as Jonah could get, God was caring for him. We read in verse 17 of chapter 1, "Now the Lord had prepared a great fish to swallow up Jonah. And Jonah was in the belly of the fish three days and three nights."

Jonah running away, God following him. God was not going to let him go, so He prepared a great fish! Could such a thing be possible? Of course it could. Why should we ever doubt it when we have a God with whom all things are possible? We should never measure God's power by our weak human standards. God had that fish there in the right spot, just in the nick of time! Oh, the never-ending love of God that works to draw us back when we go astray. Haven't you found it so at some time or other? Running away from doing God's will, but sought out and taken care of when you least deserved it.

Rebellious Jonah, for you the tide has begun to turn. Yes, but it took God's method of punishment together with His mercy to bring you back! In the most awkward situation he could ever have imagined himself, but engineered by the almighty hand of God. Remorse sets in and leads him to cry to God for deliverance! Verse 2 of chapter 2 says, "I cried by reason of mine affliction unto the Lord, and he heard me . . . all thy billows and thy waves passed over me."

Then it is that being brought down to the depths, hope begins to dawn, though tangled as it were in the weeds. Desperation was in his own soul now, and he remembered the Lord. Rebellion is being changed to remorse, but what a fruitful affliction he passed through. Hear him say in the midst of it all, "I will look again." I will turn back and seek the Lord I was fleeing from. He knew that the divine compassion would never fail him if he sought Him.

There is one more thought I want to share with you. The Lord heard his cry and spoke to the fish that He had prepared to keep Jonah in safety. At once the fish vomited him up right on to dry land. He did not even have to swim. Out of all the tangle and confusion he had been in, to a place of safety where he could begin to think again! How very gracious and wonderful the Lord is, and He is yours and mine if we know Him as Saviour.

Have you come to the place in your wanderings away from God that you can stand no more? Do you feel you want to get back to

where you were?  You know the taste of remorse, and all your
present thoughts and troubles remind you of the price you paid to
get your own way.  Well, just there is the place to look again to
the Lord that He might be gracious to you.  He will certainly bring
you up, through and out.  Don't wait for some other day, but right
now, where you are, turn to Him and let Him be your Deliverer,
bringing back peace and joy to your storm-tossed heart.  Let me
leave with you a verse to think about as you go about your day's
work:

"To obey is better than sacrifice." (*1 Sam. 15:22*)

Of course it is, and it saves a lot of heartache.


## JONAH RECOMMISSIONED

> "The word of the Lord came unto Jonah
> the second time." *Jonah 3:1*

ONE day I heard of a young boy who had a promising singing
voice, and often his parents called on him to sing before friends and
guests in the home.  He usually enjoyed the applause that he got,
but one day, when he came in from school, he noticed that there
were some people there that he had not seen before and guessed
that soon he would be called in to show off before them.  He just
was not in the mood for it and tried to sneak in quietly and hide
from his parents' watchful eyes.  Poor boy, he was not very success-
ful and, e'er long, his father called him to come and let these friends
hear him sing!

The black determined mood got really hold of him as he refused,
making all kinds of excuses, but his father could see through them
all.  Finally, he left off trying to persuade him.  In desperation, the
lad went out into the garden and tried to occupy himself with the
things that usually gave him a great deal of pleasure, but somehow
he couldn't work up any enthusiasm at all.  He determined just the
same to keep out of the way of the grown-ups.

Eventually, as the time dragged by, he decided to slip indoors
again.  Then his father appeared and looked at him.  "Dad, shall I

go in now and sing for those friends?" he asked. With a gentle pat
on his head, Father said, "Oh, no, son, you are too late. They have
gone. You have missed your opportunity."

Isn't that just what you find happening every day? You know,
when you really think about it, those words could easily have been
written over a page in the life of Jonah. Jonah, you disobeyed, and
lost your opportunity.

Ah, but, there is a very precious verse in Isaiah 42 which says,
"A bruised reed shall He not break, and the smoking flax shall He
not quench", and as we check into the life of Jonah we see God
putting it into action. Jonah looked again to the Lord and cried for
deliverance and the Merciful Lord heard and answered the plea of
his disobedient servant!

I was thinking a short while ago of a couple of people who made
known their hearts' deepest need in these words. One says, "I have
wandered so far away and am so very unhappy, please show me the
way back to God"; and the other, "Oh, that I had never strayed."
The awful price one pays for getting one's own way. Is there any
ray of hope in Jonah's story for people with such deep longings
after God?

We might easily ask, "Did he have any right to expect God to
hear his pleadings when he had deliberately chosen to go his own
way"? Well, for that matter, what right have any of us to the
divine compassion and love which restores? None at all, but He
offers it to us just the same, and with open arms receives us when we
call. Yes, there is hope for all who will return, for a broken and
contrite heart He will not despise.

In chapter 3 the Lord meets Jonah and it seems without any
argument the Lord recommissions him and tells him to "go to
Nineveh, that great city, and preach unto it the preaching that I bid
thee". God could have employed someone else to do that job, but
He chose to give him another opportunity. "Go to Nineveh." It
was not with the voice of a threatening parent, but that of a loving
Father giving him another chance.

We cannot be sure that this will always happen, but we have
comfort in the fact that God will make something of us if only we
will let Him. He might give us a different job to do, but, so long as
it is His appointment, that is all that matters.

"Jonah, just go to Nineveh and do what I ask you!" It was an arduous journey of three days, but he faced it this time. There is that great wicked city just before him, and as soon as he enters he lifts up his voice in warning lest God should destroy them for their evil ways. And you know, something happened. Conviction of sin swept over the people from the greatest to the least. The king himself stripped off his royal apparel and put on sackcloth and led his people back to God. Nothing else really mattered. Never mind how important it seemed. Even the cattle were to take second place. It must needs be that the whole city repent of their evil ways that God be merciful to them. A mighty cry went up to God as they repented. How much we wish that we could see the same thing today!

Revival blessing came to Nineveh because Jonah let his mouth be used to carry God's message. It is full of encouragement for us. When he faced his Nineveh at God's command he saw God's work. What about you and me? Who can tell how great the blessing that will flow from obedience to what God asks?

You may not have to go very far afield for your Nineveh. It could be just there in your own home, in the midst of your family and friends, and that can be hard enough sometimes. But it always pays to listen to the whispers of the Holy Spirit and seek His aid to do what He asks.

Yes, indeed, your life may be lived within the four walls of your home, the very place that God intended you to be, and He wants to make use of you. So, dear friend, as you take time to read over this chapter in the life of Jonah, and perhaps become aware of the fact that you were drifting your own way, return to Him and be assured His arms will receive you and His great love will enfold you and enable you to do what He says next.

Yes, all these things happened to Jonah so long ago, but they surely have a message for you and me in our day. Today it is brimful of hope and encouragement. Here is a closing thought for the day as we pray:

> Give me a heart, resigned, submissive, meek,
> My dear Redeemer's throne,
> Where only Christ is heard to speak,
> Where Jesus reigns alone.

# JONAH RESENTFUL

*"Doest thou well to be angry?" Jonah 4:9*

WE have seen Jonah as a man rebellious, remorseful and recommissioned. Now, in the last chapter we find him full of resentment! He saw what happened at Nineveh when he did God's bidding, and strangely enough it aroused in him the deepest feelings of resentment! It leads him to have a one-sided argument with God, the One who had shown him such wonderful compassion.

Listen to him in chapter 4, verse 2. It is just as though he were saying, "Before I fled in that boat, didn't I know that this would happen? Of course, I knew that thou art a Gracious God and merciful; slow to anger, and of great kindness and repentest Thee of the evil. I knew that Thou wouldst have mercy on them." Somehow Jonah just couldn't take it! Why should such a wicked people be allowed off, as it were, without tasting punishment? Thoughts like these flooded his mind and he gave them plenty of room, so that he was at the point where he wanted to die! His thinking was all one-sided. Since he was not at one with God in His purpose to save mankind, he would rather have seen them all wiped out.

He had not reached the place where he was able to look through God's eyes. Of course, neither had he taken into account the fact that God had actually set a time limit to His patience with the people of Nineveh. The message Jonah delivered to them was, "Yet forty days, and Nineveh shall be overthrown." If you do not repent you will pay the price in full for your mounting iniquities. Yes, there was a time limit and a warning. God gave them one more opportunity and, when He saw their true repentance, He accepted it and pardon was given. How true it is as we often sing, "He was not willing that any should perish." Yet here was his servant Jonah just about ready to give up because he did not understand the heart of God.

Doesn't it seem an unusual attitude for a servant of the Lord to have? Doing His bidding, yet indignant with His dealing with mankind. Have you ever found that sort of thing creeping into your own heart as you look around at others? Do you sometimes feel that they are unworthy of any of God's mercy, and when you see God being gracious to the returning wanderer you question why God does not punish her further to teach her a lesson? It is always possible for such a spirit to creep in, while we seek to justify our own righteous indignation, but it makes us realize how far short we come from God's standard.

The Lord had to take Jonah in hand and teach him a few things. Once again it is the hard way! He had listened to all that Jonah had to say and then asked, "Do you do well to be annoyed about what I have done?" It was a penetrating question and there was no immediate answer. He went away and sat down in the shadow of a booth just to see what God would do to that city! Once again we see so clearly revealed the loving kindness of God to His resentful child. He had prepared a great fish to save him from destruction in the first place. Now He prepares a gourd to shelter him from the heat of the day and deliver him from his grief: a gourd, a trailing plant that climbs up over the booth and gives both shelter and coolness. It reminds me of that precious verse, "A man shall be as a hiding place."

God's provision for every part of our lives! Yes, sit still, Jonah, and pay attention to what God has to say to you. Tried and tempted and even depressed you are, but not forsaken!

Have you ever noticed how God sends all kinds of gourds into our lives to protect us when we are in danger of giving in to wrong feelings and moods? Maybe a friend will come just at the moment you need her. A letter will be dropped through your letter-box that causes you to know God is thinking about you and trying to get your attention. Oh, there are so many kinds of sheltering gourds that come our way. Let's learn to recognize them! God's messengers. Then God prepared a worm to destroy the gourd. We find poor Jonah desperately mourning over its death. Just a thing that sprang up in the night. Yes, but never a tear is shed over the people of Nineveh. He just did not have things in the right perspective. Things of lesser value possessed his feelings.

Then comes the story of the strong east wind that beat upon him.

Hadn't he had enough? Yes, but God who knew his innermost needs prepared it. How long is it going to take before he sees what God is getting at? "Jonah, listen to me," says God. God had the last word. "Jonah, listen! All the things that you are so concerned about will perish. They have their day. Don't you think that, if you can have such deep feelings over passing things, I should have mercy on the six score thousand persons of Nineveh with souls that will live for ever?" And there was no answer. God had the last word. Is He having the last word in your life?

## ADORNMENT

"That they may adorn the doctrine of God our Saviour in all things." *Titus 2:10*

Do you ever do just what we call window shopping? Just having a good look and spending no money! The best time to do it is when the shops are shut, then you have time to think about what you have seen and whether or not some particular item should be purchased!

Travelling not long ago, we had an overnight stop in the lovely city of Copenhagen. It was raining quite hard and chilly, too, but we felt that we must have a walk after our trip high above the clouds, so just before bedtime we went out on the main street and walked along and looked at some of the shop windows. I remember one place in particular that had a beautiful display of their lovely fine blue china. We could not help but gaze at it, and my husband was just as fascinated as I was! It just caught your eye. Ornaments of different kinds, besides the more useful things such as table china. That window must have been an attraction to many a passer-by. I just felt that so many things would adorn any home. They would add the finishing touch to a room, and I am sure if you had been with us I would have heard you say. "Wouldn't I just love to have that! It would fit in so well with my scheme of things."

But the shops were shut and, perhaps, it was just as well. But before I went to bed that night, I made a point of scribbling down just one word, "adornment".

In Titus 2:10, when Paul was exhorting servants about their manner of living he said, "That they may adorn the doctrine of God our Saviour in all things." Adornment is something that attracts and beautifies, and it may seem strange at first to apply it to a doctrine, but the more I thought about it the more the sense of it gripped me. I realized that there is always the possibility of detracting from it rather than adorning.

When you look at a shop window you can tell at a glance if the dresser really knew his or her job. Some hold your attention, and others make a bad impression. So it is, I think, with us. How do our words and general manner of living affect others? Do we attract them by our lives as well as our words? I suppose you have often heard someone quote "People will read you when they won't read their Bibles". In other words, they expect to see you, the professing Christian, exemplify by your life what you are teaching. In the light of this it is good for us to take ourselves to task at times and ask, "Am I adorning the doctrine of God, our Saviour, in all things?" Or, "Do I just skip over some things and hope no one notices?"

How easy it is, for instance, to speak to someone else about patience, and yet show an irritability of spirit when things just don't go as you want them to! I know it is possible to speak of the peace and rest the Lord gives, and yet, as friends and neighbours look on, they see furrowed brows and anxious, worried expressions. They may sense, too, in your conversation that you are bearing your own burden as though you had no Heavenly Father who cared!

Surely, too, it is even possible to talk of love, the best of God's gifts, and yet in a time of trouble and adversity, a harsh criticism of someone else creeps into your voice as you share your opinions with another. The person listening is left wondering about the kind of doctrine you profess!

There are so many ways that we can detract from the truth and beauty of the doctrines of the Word of God, and even turn people away from the Saviour we represent.

I so well recall hearing two people one day "having it all out together" but in rather loud voices! One said to the other, "Instead of winning, you repel, in spite of the doctrines you hold. Lovely words, but your life never helps!" Those two never did really get together to my knowledge; they were poles apart. For while one was trying to adorn the very doctrines she taught, the other with a selfish unforgiving spirit went her own way believing she was right! See what I mean about adornment?

As we go about our housework, tidying up and trying to make our homes attractive to those who share them with us, let's see to it that we will always adorn the doctrine of God our Saviour in all things that we permit ourselves to do and say. Yes, people are looking at you and me and they are listening to us as well. How do we impress them as Christians? Do we attract them or do we repel? Do they really see the fruit of the Spirit in us as we talk and live with them?

The story is told of a dear old Christian lady who was once asked what she used to make her whole being so bright and attractive. She had an answer and willingly gave it. This was her answer:

> I use for my lips, truth,
> I use for my voice, kindness,
> I use for my eyes, compassion.
> I use for my hands, charity.
> I use for my figure, uprightness.
> I use for my heart, love.
> And I use for any who do not like me, prayer.

Such a person surely adorned the doctrine she professed.

I am sure that as these hearts of ours are surrendered to the Lord, He, by His Spirit, will help us to attract others to Him. If we have His adorning in our lives, everything about us will speak of Him. There is a lovely prayer summed up in the words of a well-loved hymn which we can make ours today:

> I want that adorning Divine,
> That only my God can bestow.
> I want in those beautiful garments to shine
> That mark out Thy household below.

# TELEPHONES

"Let us come boldly unto the throne of
grace . . ." *Hebrews 4:16*

RING, went the telephone one day recently. There are times when a phone can be really frustrating. Wrong numbers at awkward times! Messages for other people just when you can't go and get them. Then there is the type of person who likes to sit and chatter at the other end and waste your time. You are wishing she would ring off and let you get on with your work! Yes, there are all sorts of troublesome things about a phone, but I think most of us would agree that it really is a most useful device. Sometimes we wonder how we ever got on without it. Emergencies crop up in every household, and what a blessing it is to be able to dial the number you want to get immediate help! Many miles of travel can be saved, too, through a telephone call. Of course, there is always the joy of being able to talk with loved ones who are far away.

We had just finished our evening meal when our phone rang. The operator said, "Hold the line for a long distance call." Eventually through the wires and lots of noises and voices the connections were made, and a well-known voice said, "This is the fourth time I have tried to get you, but at last we have made it." Then when my husband was talking, I began thinking about our lines of communication with God. It suddenly struck me that this friend had met with great difficulty in getting through to us with an important message. But we as Christians have an open line of communication with the Lord and a lasting invitation to use it at all times. There is someone who intercedes for us. One who has passed this way and is touched with the feelings of our infirmities. The verse of Scripture that came to my mind was Hebrews 4:16, "Let us therefore come boldly unto the throne of grace, that we may obtain mercy, and find grace to help in time of need."

Earthly thrones are forbidding to most of us, but, wonderful thought, here is one that welcomes. You as a Christian can get

through at once to the throne of grace and there will never be anyone to tell you that the line is busy or that the number is engaged,
however many people are petitioning the Lord at the same time!
That is a wonderful thing. You can have a personal hearing, and
be assured of an understanding heart that hears your request. The
invitation is to come boldly! Come without hesitancy! You
won't even have to wait for someone else to put you through! So
come with your requests and family concerns.

On God's side the line is always clear. But, of course, we do well
to remember that it could be on our side that the line is blocked
through something in our lives that is not pleasing to Him. Or, as
we read in Psalm 66:18, "If I regard iniquity in my heart, the Lord
will not hear me." Just there, in the quiet of your kitchen or
wherever you are, learn the joy of having swift communication
with your Lord, and prove the blessedness of His immediate help
in every circumstance.

As I went on thinking about this telephone call, I remembered
that it had two-way traffic. My husband was doing quite a bit of
listening to the voice at the other end and writing down notes on
the pad beside him. I thought, yes, we don't do all the talking, we
want to hear what the other person has to say. It is just the same
when we come to God. We want to talk to Him, but He has things
that He wants to communicate to us. We must listen to His voice.
Years ago we used to sing a lovely hymn and one of the verses read:

Oh, give me Samuel's ear, the open ear, O Lord,
Alive and quick to hear each whisper of Thy word,
Like him to answer at Thy call and to obey Thee first of all.

Through the reading of God's word He will communicate with us,
and make His commands and wishes known. Through it we will
hear the voice that tells us the next thing to do. We will discern
the voice of love that cheers and encourages us.

Then, of course, God may want to communicate His message
through us to others! It simply means that we have to be ready to
hear and obey. I think of the Apostle Paul of whom we read in
Acts 16 that he was being directed by the Holy Spirit as to where he
should go. Some doors were closed, but Paul heard the voice
which said, "Come over into Macedonia, and help us." Because

he was in the position where he heard and obeyed, God communicated to others through him and the course of history was changed!

We can also read in Acts 8 of Philip, who was in the midst of revival scenes, but he heard the voice of the Lord telling him to leave it all and go down to the desert. He obeyed, and once again we read of how God used him to communicate His message to the Ethiopian eunuch who was waiting for someone to interpret to him the message of Isaiah 53. It was the message of the Saviour.

Does the Lord whisper a message to your heart today as He did to mine? Christian friend, have you been bothered about many things these days, and have you talked a good deal with others about the things that trouble? Why not just now heed the invitation of the Lord and come without any delay to the throne of grace where you will meet with Him and find all that you need in Him? If you are conscious that you have been doing all the talking and not giving Him a chance to communicate with you, then be restful in His presence and let Him say what He wants to. Let Him bid you go or stay!

Can you carry away into your kitchen and through your home today the words of the old hymn:

> In the secret of His presence how my soul delights to hide,
> Oh, how precious are the lessons that I learn at Jesus' side.

## FRET NOT!

"Fret not . . ." *Psalm 37:1*

THE other day when I was washing out some tea-cloths, I suddenly remembered that years ago a friend put the question to me, "What is it that is so freely given, but so rarely accepted?" The more I searched for the correct answer, the more complicated it became. I just could not satisfy her and in the end had to admit defeat. "You tell me," I said. With a sparkle in her eye, she looked me full in the face, happy that she had puzzled me and then she uttered the one word, "Advice!"

"Ach," I said, "Why couldn't I think of that, for it is so very true!" I know that there are times in all of our lives when advice is offered on every hand by well-meaning people! Do this, or don't do that, whatever happens, they say. Some even go as far as saying, "Take my advice for what it is worth." Already you know full well that it is not worth much for she has not faced the thing that you are going through. She has not walked your way. To do what she suggests would end in disaster for you. On the other hand, how very welcome is the counsel and advice of a mature person who knows what she is talking about.

While I was washing those tea-cloths, I had been thinking about the advice David gives to us in Psalm 37. The very fact that he was one with years of life behind him, rich in maturity and the things of God, makes us want to turn our ears over to him and listen to what he has to say. There in that very opening verse he hits us hard with just a couple of words, "Fret not!" They make you sit up and think right away! But, David, haven't you ever had cause to fret? Didn't circumstances sometimes make you want to complain? Ah, yes, he says, but it is so futile! You do not gain anything by fretting. I have found a better way.

Let's look at it again. "Fret not thyself because of evil doers, neither be thou envious against the workers of iniquity. For they shall soon be cut down like the grass, and wither as the green herb." He had learned the uselessness of wearing himself out physically and spiritually over things that he could not change, but he had found that God could, so why the need for fretting?

"Fret not because of evil doers", and all the way through the Psalm he refers to people as being the cause of so much fret! It is true. That other person with all her scheming seems to get away with it. How can she act like it, we say, and yet appear to prosper? You keep thinking about her and comparing yourself with her and eventually it starts eating into you like a cancer. It is a constant source of irritation. In the end you fret so much that you become a hard person to live with. Folk don't want to meet you because they know exactly what you are going to start talking about!

That is what fretting does to one, and it makes you thoroughly discontented. Some particular thing about someone else nags and gnaws at you. You take it to bed with you and get up with it in the morning worse than ever. "Fret not thyself because of evil doers."

D

You read those words and suddenly you are pulled up with a jolt! Fret not because of those who imagine mischief against you. They won't prosper for ever. Their time for that sort of thing is limited.

I don't know the reason for your particular fret, but some people have to live in circumstances that are not easy. Hannah, the mother of Samuel, was one such, but she learned how to stop fretting when she prayed, when she took it to the Lord. Fretting is like a poison that permeates every bit of you and colours your words and actions. Our beloved Psalmist does not just say "fret not" and leave you in mid-air, but he had a wonderful antidote to offer you. Of course, however, a medicine must be taken if it is to have any effect!

"Get out of yourself," he says. "Stop fretting, and trust in the Lord, who is greater far than all that is against you." Go ahead and do good and recognize from this very moment that God is able to look after all your concerns. Trust in the Lord and do good, and verily thou shalt be fed! You won't have any need to worry for He will be sufficient for everything. He will give you the spiritual nourishment that you need, as well as take care of your affairs.

Turn your thoughts deliberately away from the things that have been making you fret, and "delight thyself also in the Lord, and he shall give thee the desires of thine heart". It stands to reason that if God is your delight, your desires will be right ones! You know, friend, when you give the Lord His rightful place in your life, the fretting will cease. It just can't live when He is in control and your chief joy!

Making the Lord your delight will take the wrinkles from your brow and the pout from your lips, and give sleep to your eyes. If that is not a recipe for beauty, what is?

Trust in the Lord and do good. "Delight thyself also in the Lord." The third pill to swallow is, "Commit thy way unto the Lord; trust also in him; and he shall bring it to pass." It sounds like a sugar-coated one, doesn't it? Ah, but it is sweet all the way through right to the very end! Hand it over to Him, and let Him do the impossible thing for you. He will see to it that you are exonerated if folk have been blaming you wrongfully. You will have no regrets.

God is never baffled as we are. He shall bring it to pass. There is no vindication equal to that which the Lord gives. Are you finding it hard to commit your way to Him? Haven't you committed the keeping of your soul to Him and never doubted? Well, can't He take care of the things of your life as well? Of course He can!

Just one more dose of medicine before we go. Verse 7 says: "Rest in the Lord, and wait patiently for him." Fret not because of . . . because of what? You know your answer. Be quiet before the Lord and let His rest invade your whole being and remember that the steps of a good man or woman are ordered by the Lord. He will suffice!


## CORNERS OF THE WAY

"The God of my mercy shall prevent me."
*Psalm 59:10*

My reading of another Psalm recently very vividly reminded me of an occasion when I was going to visit a friend in a district that was quite new to me. She gave me all kinds of instructions as to how to reach her home, which was out in the country. I usually have what we call "a good bump for locality" and it does not bother me much to go and find places. This time it did, however, as the directions seemed so intricate. I really did wonder if I would find it!

"Just ask the bus conductor to let you off at such and such a corner," she said. "Then turn left until you reach the crossroads. Then right until you come to a large farm house, then . . ." On and on it went! I scribbled it down, but before the day came I found myself just full of all kinds of "supposes".

Bus conductors have lots to think about, and suppose he forgot to let me off at the right place. Where would that land me? One suppose led to another until I did not feel too happy at the prospect before me. Then, just hours before I was to set out to the bus depot, our friend the postman called and dropped a letter through the box for me. Recognizing the handwriting, I quickly tore it open, and this is what I read:

"Dear Norah, I have decided to come and meet you at the corner where the bus stops, so when you reach there about 10.30 a.m., just keep your eyes open for me. I will be waiting to bring you home!"

What a difference it made! In a flash away went all my "suppose tensions", and I was able to enjoy the trip. And, sure enough, as my watch ticked around to 10.30, the bus stopped and I spotted my friend waiting at the corner. We laughed together as I told her my story, but you know the fact that she came to meet me made all the difference.

In Psalm 59 we find David once again in a tight place, hardly knowing which way to turn. He was being unjustly accused on every hand. His enemies gave him no rest by day or night. They were determined to run him to earth, as it were, and that not because of any sin or transgression on his part. He weighs it all up, and then this man, who gives such wonderful help to others in their darkest and trying hours, turns both his situation and his enemies over to the Lord. He determines within himself to wait on the Lord, knowing full well that God would be his defence! He would stand between them, and if God stood there, what harm could they do to him?

Yes, see how he recognizes God's power in the time of his own weakness. There was simply nothing better that he could do but to put God right there in the midst of the strife of tongues and jealousies that surrounded him.

Then in verse 10 came the words that so blessed my own heart as I pondered them. "The God of my mercy shall prevent me." "Prevent" is an old word used there which really means to "go before". So it reads, "The God of my mercy shall go before me". He will be in front and I will follow.

Then I found another translation or paraphrase of this verse that just seems to fit right into our very lives. Here it is: "My God with His loving kindness shall meet me at every corner of the way." Now you know why I remembered my earlier experience! "Every corner of the way." David was not going to push ahead in his own strength and fight it out and let his enemies know that he was right. No, God could do that far better for him! He had an inner persuasion that the God of his mercy was well able to take care of him and deal with the things that came his way. It would be the natural answer to take things into his own hands and vindicate his honour, but because he knew that God would meet him at every corner of the way, he would wait for Him. "Lord, You take over," he says, "and I will wait."

Then listen as he closes his Psalm with a note of praise and thanksgiving. "I will sing of Thy power; yea, I will sing aloud of Thy mercy in the morning." Waiting on the Lord always produces praise!

Dear friend, how do you stand today? Are you hemmed in by things that are hard to understand? Is your mind full of what we might call "spiritual supposes" as you face some new experience? You wonder how you will ever manage to face it? You take a look round and it fills your heart with dismay because you see no way out. You seem to be always coming to corners that are blind. However much you try, you just can't see what is ahead. You find yourself baffled and just about ready to give up. Looking at yourself in the mirror, you find the lines deepening on your forehead as you concentrate on your problems. Where will it all lead to?

It was F. W. Boreham who once wrote, "Give God time, and even when Pharaoh's host is on Israel's heels a path through the waters will be suddenly open." "Give God time, and when the bed of the brook is dry Elijah shall hear the guiding voice."

Of course it is so. It could not be otherwise when God is your defence! So wait on Him and open up the windows of your heart today, even if all around looks black, because He is ready to meet you with His loving kindness at every corner of the way.

It is such a wonderful verse, laden with help and blessing to weary hearts. Here you can find succour, strength and solace for your way. The knowledge that the One who has redeemed you by His blood stands between you and the tempter, that He is never baffled, and will never leave you to fight your own way through, should put a song into your heart and brighten up your day.

"My God with His loving kindness shall meet me at every corner of the way", and, may I add, even today!

> Are you standing at Wits End corner,
> Christian with troubled brow?
> Are you thinking of all that's before you,
> And all you are bearing now?
> Does all the world seem against you,
> And you in the battle alone?
> Remember at Wits End corner,
> Is just where God's power is shown.

# DOWN IN THE VALLEY

"Who passing through the valley of
Baca make it a well." *Psalm 84: 6*

I WAS busy with my usual household jobs one day, wiping the dust
off a chair, and was suddenly conscious of the fact that I was humming over an old hymn tune that I had not heard for a long time:

> Down in the valley with my Saviour I would go,
> Where the storms are sweeping and the dark waters flow.
> With His hand to lead me I will never never fear,
> Dangers cannot fright me if my Lord is near.

I can remember singing those words with real depths of feeling
years ago and meaning every bit of it, but I did not realize all that
might be involved in the following of the Lord through each day
and into the years! Little did I know that there were going to be
times when the waters would be dark, and fierce the storm. Yes,
perhaps, it was comparatively easy to sing it when all was calm and
bright, but the times came when those words held a distinct challenge for me, when I was up against it. But looking back today, I
remember, too, the way the Lord brought me through! He dealt
with all the fears and proved Himself to be enough for all my need.

I suppose I really got to thinking about this hymn and the experiences of life because I had been reading again in Psalm 84. It held a
real message for me, and I hope as I share my thoughts with you that
they will be a means of encouragement to you for today. In verses
five to seven we read, "Blessed is the man whose strength is in thee;
in whose heart are the ways of them. Who passing through the
valley of Baca make it a well; the rain also filleth the pools. They
go from strength to strength."

The Psalmist speaks of the longing heart seeking and finding God.
Of the trusting heart going from strength to strength, and of the
upright heart from whom God will withhold no good thing. But
right there in the middle of it is a little phrase that often touches

your life and mine! It says of those trusting folk "who passing through the valley of Baca make it a well". This is usually interpreted as "a place of tears", but they were just passing through, not staying there all the time. It was just an episode in the journey of life.

Yes, they were seeking, trusting and praising the Lord, but they were permitted to know the experience of passing through the valley of tears and at the end life was richer for them. We read that "passing through" they made it a well! Water always speaks of life!

Have you ever looked at a valley all dried up and barren through lack of water, and then transferred your gaze to the one that has known the clouds and the mists and drank in the heavy rains? Oh, it is so refreshing to the eye. Verdant pasture land, profitable to all. A place of beauty and attraction! And that is what God is after in your life when He leads you through the valley of tears. He is purposing to bring fruit that will remain and bless out of your present experience, however difficult it may seem to be now.

I know full well that you will come up against the hard places as you seek to follow the Lord, maybe even there in your home, but your Lord knows all about it. The tears shed or unshed. There will be the things that hurt and bruise. Unexpected thorns and briars. They may strike at you from people of whom you least expect it. Loyalty to the Lord might leave you in a lonely spot, but always He will be with you as you pass through your valley of tears. There are the burdens and cares which have fallen upon you. You weep over the sins and sorrows of others. Your tears are not those of self-pity, but concern. Dear friend, the Valley of Tears is not meant to be a stopping place for you, just an experience from which the Lord is seeking to bring fruitfulness into your life.

I once heard a very dear friend of mine pray when she lost her husband, "Oh, Lord, don't let this be a lost sorrow to me." Life had taught her something, hadn't it? Your experience, too, can be turned to a valley of blessing. You will look again to the Lord and dry your eyes and wonder at His marvellous grace and patience. That old hymn has another verse which says:

Down in the valley with my Saviour I would go,
Where the flowers are blooming and the sweet waters flow.

Through your temptations, trials and tears God will lead you on from strength to strength and show you greater things. The sun will break through for you as you walk close beside Him.

There are lots of valleys to be crossed as we journey along, and even if we come to the one we speak of as the valley of the shadow, we need have no fear, for He is with us and will take us safely through to glory! What an exchange that will be! Then for a moment I was thinking there will be no dark valley when Jesus comes to gather His loved ones home!

Every valley will be transformed if we learn to walk through it trusting the promise of His Presence!

## SPOT OR WRINKLE

"Not having spot, or wrinkle, or any such thing." *Ephesians* 5: 27

Does this happen to be washing-day for you? I will try and not hinder you too long, but I thought you might be interested to know what happened to me on a certain wash-day! I got the clothes all washed and hung up to dry. As I went about doing other things, I kept hoping that I would get through as I had planned in my own mind! You know how you make a mental note of what you want to do and try to keep to it, but it is not always possible. Well, it turned out for me that I did get the clothes dry. As I do not use a steam iron, I damped them all down and rolled them up, saying to myself, "This will be my first job tomorrow."

Sure enough, after I had cleared up the breakfast things, I got out my ironing-board and plugged in the iron. What a blessing it is to have an electric iron! I always like to get the hard things done first and out of the way. Then I feel relieved as I look at the clock and see how the time is passing. I shook out the first garment, and it seemed that I had rolled a thousand creases into it. I wondered what kind of a job I would make of it! Backwards and forwards went the iron, between buttons and all the little intricate bits, and eventually

I held it up, fairly well pleased with the result of my effort at transformation. So, I went on to the next thing. Then my mind got busy on a verse of Scripture.

I am so thankful that in my early years I learned Scripture by heart, for now it comes readily to my mind when I am working. I had washed out the stains from table linen, and now as I ironed out the wrinkles and creases I suddenly thought, "Yes, what a job God has with us to make us what He wants us to be." The verses that came so clearly to my mind were, "Christ loved the church, and gave himself for it, that he might sanctify and cleanse it with the washing of water by the word, that he might present it to himself a glorious church, not having spot, or wrinkle, or any such thing; but that it should be holy and without blemish." What a purpose He has and what a standard He has given to us. As I pushed that iron over the tablecloth, my heart was lifted up in gratitude to God for His wonderful love.

So great a Saviour and salvation. Sufficient for the past, the present and the future. My feet lost their tiredness as I stood there, and my soul was refreshed. Christ loved you and me and gave Himself for us. Stained in sin without a remedy until He shed His precious Blood to make us fit to share eternity with Him. Doesn't it thrill your heart as it does mine to know and rejoice in the fact that "Sin stains are lost in that life giving flow"? "Nothing could for sin atone, nothing but the blood of Jesus." I can't always get the stains out of my washing, but there is no sin stain too deeply dyed for Him. What a Saviour! The purpose of His cleansing? To present us a glorious church not having spot or wrinkle or any such thing!

As my rolled-up pile of washing decreased and the neatly folded articles looked back at me, I thought of that expression "Without spot or wrinkle or any such thing". There were some things that needed only a warm iron, and very slight pressure to get them smooth. For others, however, I had to switch on the iron to hot and apply more weight with my hand. You know what I mean, don't you? Some things are delicate and easily scorched. Here again I thought of all of God's dealings in love with us to make us what He wants us to be. Some of us are filled with wrinkles and not a bit attractive, but the Lord knows just how and where to apply the pressure. He know how much furnace heat it is going to take until He can see His image clear in us, and He stands by, ready to turn off the heat when He is satisfied.

Then some of us have rough edges about us and the Lord wants these things smoothed out. If heat doesn't do it, He finds some other way of correcting that thing. That reminds me, a few days ago, I dropped my iron on the tiled floor and without noticing it chipped a piece off the point. Next time I was ironing, I couldn't make out why the clothes were getting scratched until I turned the iron over. My husband took a look at it and said, "I can fix that for you." He filed it back and forth, and soon the iron was gliding smoothly over a starched collar! The file was the instrument used to do away with the sharp edge!

Have you ever been concerned about the unpleasant bits in yourself, and you have asked the Lord to deal with them? Then watch His methods. It is interesting. I know, for I have done it many times! He knows best how to get rid of the wrinkles and deal with the rough places that make you hard to get on with!

I am so thankful that it is His hand that holds the iron or the file! He knows just how much pressure to apply and maybe the things that you are calling afflictions are just God's ways of answering your prayers! Job said once, "When He hath tried me I shall come forth as gold."

Dear friend, if you are asking Him to take the wrinkles out of your life, lie still in His hand and let Him use the methods He chooses, for He wants you to be part of a glorious church! No spot or wrinkle or any such thing.

I finished my ironing and went to the kitchen, but I hope your next washing- and ironing-day will bring you a blessing too!

# I FORGOT

". . . and will not remember my sins."
*Isaiah 43: 25*

I HEARD myself say a few days ago, "Oh, I forgot." I went shopping and forgot to take with me the list I had so carefully prepared to save my time at the grocer's. I know that you do the same thing sometimes, so I don't feel too badly about it!

"Oh, I forgot." It is a common enough phrase, and we hear it so very often. Sometimes in sincerity and sometimes, I'm afraid, as an excuse. "Oh, I forgot to post that letter, and I have carried it about in my handbag for the last two days." "I forgot to get those flowers for Mrs. Smith, and she would have so much enjoyed them!" "Oh, those eggs I meant to get to make the cake to take to Mary. I forgot!" And what seems worse to any housewife is when she has to say after the cake is in the oven, "I forgot to put the baking powder in."

Tragedy, it seems. I heard a friend say one day not long ago, "I have got a good forgettory." Well, some things don't matter too much. But there are some forgetfulnesses that make us embarrassed. Some things can be remedied, but others can't. Don't you find that there are always things that you would like to really forget, but somehow you can't? They nag at you and won't leave you alone.

You know the sort of thing that I mean. It would be such a relief if I could forget the rashly spoken word that so badly hurt someone else, or that letter that ought never to have been written, much less posted. The whisper that went around and brought a sad look to the face of the one being whispered about. She knew all the time! Oh, if I could only forget how an action of mine hindered someone else. And so it goes.

Not too long ago my husband and I were staying with some friends in the beautiful city of Edinburgh. At lunch-time one day our host was telling us of someone who told of a man in deep concern because he could not forget his former sins. Oh, yes, he had asked the Lord to forgive him, and was trusting in the precious blood of the Saviour, but somehow he just could not forget his past life and was daily robbed of the sweetness of God's peace. His sins were always before him.

The man of God in whom he confided listened to his story and said, "Ah, but that is just the difference between you and God. You can't forget, but when God forgives, He forgets." Let me read to you what He said in Isaiah 43:25, "I, even I, am He that blotteth out thy transgressions for mine own sake, and will not remember thy sins."

One day you will stand before God and want to say to Him, "I am so sorry for the sins I committed," and He will say to you, "What sins? I had forgotten! They are cast into the depths of the sea."

I sat at the table eating and enjoying my food, but I was digesting the wonder of that thought. My sins which were many have been blotted out, forgotten by God, not with a careless indifference but with a loving, holy forgetfulness in the great mercy of God. That was a rich lunch for me that day.

Love that covers and forgets the ugly thing called sin that nailed the Son of God to the Cross, and in that very Cross was manifest a love so strong and enduring. Blessed forgetfulness. Next time you hear yourself say, "Oh, I forgot," just recall what it is that God forgets when you turn from your sin and let Him in to dwell!

Ah, but, I thought, there is another side to it. He forgets the sin I have repented of and forsaken, but He does not forget me, His child. It is not in the nature of God to forget those whom He has redeemed! In that wonderful book of Isaiah (49:15) I read, "Can a woman forget her sucking child, that she should not have compassion on the son of her womb? Yea, they may forget, yet will I not forget thee." Spoken of a people, yes, but also His word to you and me!

Can a mother forget her offspring? It seems impossible, but it can be so in this fickle world in which we live. How many a child today bemoans the fact that mother forgot her, forsook her and left her alone. What longing and sorrow of heart it brings! A friend wrote to me recently and mentioned that in her childhood she was sent away to another family to be cared for, but all the longing of her young heart was for her mother. No one could make up for that loss. Later she found the Lord as her Saviour and followed Him. Today, a lonely widow at 77 years of age, she is full of praise for God's faithfulness. Never forgotten, never forsaken by Him.

Can a mother forget? Yes, she may, but God's eternal promise to you and me is, "I will not forget thee." He is thinking about you, just now as you read this book. I wonder if you are one of those women prone to think that, because your lot is hard and lonely, God has forgotten about you? Dear friend, don't let such a thought take root in your heart and mind; reject it as you would poison.

Even a sparrow is not forgotten of God. Forgetfulness may be a great sin on our part, but we can never accuse our wonderful Lord of such a thing. Have you been doubting Him? Doubt no more, but rejoice in His thought for you. And now I close with these lovely words I used to hear my mother sing so often:

> Sweet is the promise, I will not forget thee.
> Nothing can molest or turn my soul away,
> Even though the night be dark within the valley,
> Just beyond is shining an Eternal day.

> I will not forget thee or leave thee.

## FORGETTING MY TOIL

> "God hath made me forget all my toil."
> *Genesis 41:51*

LAST time I closed with a verse of that lovely old hymn from Alexander's book, number 118:

> Sweet is the promise, I will not forget thee.

I am coming back to it because it really set my thoughts in motion! The last verse says:

> When at the golden portals I am standing,
> All my tribulation, all my sorrow past,
> How sweet to hear the blessed proclamation,
> Enter faithful servant, welcome home at last.

To the soul that has endured the fires of affliction down here those will be precious words, indeed. I have the utmost feeling for people who have to go the hard way. Countless thousands of people are suffering today in a manner that most of us have never experienced. Yet, how easily we succumb to the slightest thing!

I was talking to a friend of mine one day about happenings that had a crushing effect upon her because they were so unjust, but she smiled and said, "Oh, that is all past history. I have learned to live and forget. The Lord has taken care of those things.'

It led me to think about Joseph. What suffering he endured both mental and physical. Separated from his parents, sold, unjustly accused, cast into prison, unwanted and, yes, forgotten. Forgotten even by those whom he had considered. As a young man, he tested in full the anguish of loneliness, but there in the midst of it all, we are reminded that God was with him! With him, not merely as a looker-on, but as the Almighty who was going to do great things for him, with him and through him. So it was that through all the changing scenes of his life, the day came when he was released from prison and given a place of honour and authority. God had not forgotten.

In Genesis 41:51 we read that "Joseph called the name of his firstborn Manasseh: For God, said he, hath made me forget all my toil, and all my father's house." God hath made me forget all my toil. If ever there was a blessed forgetfulness in the life of a human being, it is surely expressed just there. It is just as though he were saying, "God hath caused me to forget, put out of my heart and mind all the malice, sorrow and disgrace that was meted out to me so unworthily, because He has given so much more than I lost."

Seeing the vindicating hand of God in his life turned his eyes away from the things that he had suffered so ruthlessly from his very own family and others. God has done so much for me, and now as he looks at his son whose very name means "forgetting", there is a constant reminder that although he was forgotten and forsaken by men, he proved the truth of "I will not forget thee".

"Forget all my toil and all my father's house." Instead of harping back with criticisms and unkind words, he forgets. Does that thought bite into your own heart today? You have been dwelling on the things that people have done to you, the injustices, the slander, the hurts and the slights. Oh, yes, you know all about such things for you have felt them like a lance, and they leave such a bitter taste.

Dear Christian friend, your Lord has so much more to offer you, and you can put Him to the test as did Joseph. If only you will deliberately turn yourself and your trouble-making circumstances over to Him, He will see you through and make you rich in His grace, the grace that covers and puts away those unpleasant things. Why, just at this moment I can recall some trying experiences of my own that once filled my horizon, but they don't hurt or trouble any longer. Why? Because God gave me so much more than I thought I was losing!

Then I notice, too, that when Joseph's second son was born, he called him Ephraim, for he said, "God hath caused me to be fruitful in the land of my affliction." Just right there in the land of my troubles God hath made me fruitful!

What a wonderful uplift for you if the day is dark with troubles. Maybe you feel like running away from it all. You just can't stand the strain any longer, but I expect that what would happen if you did is that you would take your burdens with you and go on remembering! Running away is not the solution. Even if you feel it is almost the last straw. Right here, says Joseph, in the place of my affliction God meets with me and makes me fruitful!

Have you any idea what God is after in that life of yours? It is His plan and desire for you that you bring forth fruit. This very thing that is pressing so hard upon you, put over into His hands, can prove to be the thing that will bring to you the greatest blessing and fruitfulness that will enrich so many others. Even just now you can talk with the Lord and tell Him all about the things that are souring your life and robbing you of the sweetness of His grace. For I know that remembering that sort of thing narrows and spoils one's life.

Ask Him to show you how to forget the unlovely things and produce in you the fruit that will make you a radiant Christian before you ever get to the glory. Let's walk together by God's grace the way of forgetfulness towards the things that might have been meant for evil, but which God means for our good. When you learn to pray for those who despitefully use you, you can't help but forget. Try it. Now back to work, with a big God bless you!

# BUT GOD

". . . But God . . ." *Genesis 50: 20*

It was a letter that took my mind off the job that I was doing and made me think of the story of Joseph. The writer was a mother who suddenly found herself plunged into one of those dark tunnels through which Christians sometimes pass. Until that day, hers had been a happy home with the Lord at its head. But that cruel blow struck without any warning and she was engulfed in a great sorrow. It has been a long tunnel for her, and the end is not yet in sight. But, oh, how I was struck by her undaunted trust and faith in God in the midst of such trying circumstances. She commits each day to the Lord and has proved that He never fails her and He enables her to face life with Him. Looking to the future, she said, "I dreaded . . . but God . . ." That is what made the difference. "But God . . ." Even with a sore heart she is learning to live in the realm of the supernatural.

There was another who found great comfort in those two words and was able to use them as he looked back on a difficult way. In the book of Genesis, chapter 50 and verse 20, you find Joseph facing those of his own family who had been the cause of all his trouble and saying to them, "As for you, ye thought evil against me; but God meant it unto good."

What a triumph that was. Joseph, the owner of the coat of many colours, the loved son of his parents, sent on an errand to his brothers, never returned, but at their cruel hands was thrown into a pit. Afterwards he was sold to some passing traders and later unjustly accused and cast into prison and forgotten of men. Surely that was enough to make anyone feel there was no hope of deliverance.

In most people it would have stirred up a desire for revenge and vindication, but Joseph committed it all to God and was prepared to wait His time. Faithful even in prison, his attitude brought him some recognition and he was given the custody of two prisoners whom Pharaoh had put there. He cared for them, and just there he was used of God to interpret their dreams which eventually were used towards his release. There was God using circumstances that seemed so trivial. Just a dream that bothered these men. Ah, but the Lord was with Joseph and was causing all things to work together for good. God had other plans for him and here they were being fulfilled through a stay in prison!

What a tremendous vindication God gave to him. He was ultimately freed, given a place of honour and trust, and became a succourer of many, even of those who had treated him so badly. Yes, he looks back and with love in his heart for those brothers he says, "Don't be afraid. You thought evil against me, BUT GOD deemed otherwise, He meant it unto good."

Is there a sorely tried woman reading just now? You are puzzled by the things that have been happening to you? You have felt the lash of a cruel tongue opened against you unjustly? You have known the feeling of utter helplessness when others have turned against you out of sheer jealousy? Your heart is sore because you have been let down by those you loved and trusted? Maybe the language of your heart just now as you sit and survey your life is "All these things are against me". There seems to be no answer and no end in sight and you long for understanding. Everything has got on top of you and you feel you cannot stand any longer being shunned and misjudged.

Is it possible that you have wrapped yourself up in a garment of self-pity because you have been so hurt that you have missed the greatest blessing the Lord wanted to bring into your life through these very circumstances? Look how fruitful Joseph became because he let God engineer his circumstances for him and give the reply to those who had hurt him. All the way along it was "But God".

Why don't you today commit your cause to Him and let Him bring blessing out of adversity for you? You know when we touch things ourselves and try to work out a solution that will justify us we make a mess of it, but God's vindications are worth waiting for. He will do the exceeding abundant for you and those things that are pricks and thorns today cannot harm you if you will hand them over to the Lord. Instead of the brier shall come up the myrtle!

E

I am sure that, as you pass things over to the Lord, the Holy Spirit will leave you in no doubt about what your attitude should be, for God has one great big ALTERNATIVE. That is, "Love your enemies, do good to them which hate you." Too hard for you? Put God to the test and prove Him faithful, enriching your life with a fullness you never thought possible.

> Thus wholly mastered and possessed by God,
> Forth from thy life, spontaneous and free,
> Shall flow a stream of tenderness and grace,
> Loving, because God loved, eternally.

## MIRACLES

". . . What hast thou in the house?"
*2 Kings 4: 2*

"THAT is something, the day of miracles is not passed!" Haven't you heard that expression when something out of the ordinary has happened? It makes you prick up your ears, doesn't it, and makes you want to find out what has taken place! The fact is that it comes as a big surprise, for we have really relegated the day of miracles to the back of our minds. We live in a world of tangible things, doing the everyday routine jobs, and, of course, a miracle is something out of the ordinary.

Let's look at an incident in the life of a woman in the Bible. She was suddenly going to find that there was an extraordinary side to life. Instead of the dull routine, she was going to see a miracle worked just for her. We read her story in 2 Kings 4. Let us just look at the practical side of it as it touches you and me. I am sure that God intends to speak to us when we are confronted with burdens that we cannot bear alone.

She was a widow, and that meant that she would be missing her husband in many ways. She was left with two children and was poor. Her husband had been a man who feared the Lord, but he had left a debt that had to be paid. Now the creditor comes demanding payment, and threatens to take her sons if the money is not forthcoming. Can't you imagine the feelings of dread in the heart of that mother as she realizes that she has nothing to pay with? Whatever will she do?

Turning these things over in her mind, she decides to go to Elisha, the man of God, and tell her trouble. He had time to listen to her with an understanding heart. He was full of sympathy for her. "What do you have in your house?" he asks. "All I have is a pot of oil, and that will not pay his bill."

Then the miracle begins! He tells her to do a strange thing. "Go, borrow thee vessels abroad of all thy neighbours, even empty vessels; borrow not a few. And when thou art come in, thou shalt shut the door upon thee and upon thy sons, and shalt pour out into all those vessels, and thou shalt set aside that which is full." Vessels that were empty. Acting in implicit faith, however strange it appeared to be, she did just that. Faith became sight as she saw those vessels being filled one by one. A miracle of supply in God's way happened before her very eyes. "Now," says Elisha, "go and sell it and pay your debt and live!" How the heart of that mother must have rejoiced as she realized God's care for her!

Do you think that God can take care of you? Maybe as a Christian mother you, too, are facing financial difficulties. Others do not know about them, and you hesitate to let your needs be made known. Have you ever really shut the door on yourself and family and together told the Lord all about your needs? You as His child are His responsibility and He has promised to look after you. He may not choose to meet your need in the way He did for that poor widow woman, but supply it He will if you will trust Him.

I have had many experiences of proving the Lord this way as a missionary. He never did fail. Are you burdened with the thought of where the rent money will come from, or how you will ever have enough money to feed and clothe the family? Do you recall that when there were thousands of hungry people following the Lord, He worked a miracle to feed them? The disciples said, "Send them away that they may go and buy bread." But He whose heart was filled with compassion said, "They need not depart," and He fed them just there out of the little that was on hand! At the end there was an abundance!

This same Jesus is concerned about you and will honour your
trust in Him. Your heart will rejoice as never before when you
prove Him. I remember reading a story a long time ago about two
little children who were alone and hungry. They had been
neglected. This night there was a storm raging outside as those two
children huddled together inside praying, "Give us this day our
daily bread." Outside a man took refuge in the partly opened door,
sheltering for a while from the wind and rain. He heard the prayer
of those little children and shortly afterwards, very quietly, a loaf of
bread was pushed inside the door. The children jumped to get it
and looked at it in amazement. How did it get there? Who put it
there? "Yes," they said, "we have just prayed 'Give us this day
our daily bread' and God has supplied it already!" Together they
thanked the Lord for His provision for them.

Do you think that your case is too difficult? Then remind yourself
again today that there is nothing impossible with God, dear friend.
Bring your needs to Him and remember:

> It may not be my way, it may not be thy way,
> But in some way or other the Lord will provide.

When you were a sinner and had nothing to pay your debt with,
Jesus paid it all. You can trust Him to provide for your everyday
living.


## PENINNAH THE PROVOKER

> "Let us consider one another to provoke
> unto love and to good works." *Hebrews*
> *10:24*

TODAY let's talk about a topic of interest to all women generally—
people. How many different types of people we meet with during
the day! Some quick, others slow, some practical, and others just
the opposite. Some neat and tidy, and others who do not seem to
care. Some sad and some glad. We could multiply them, but I
really have one person in mind. I have met her on different occa-

sions and found her again in reading the story of Hannah in 1 Samuel 1.

Her name is Peninnah. She was a woman who had no grace in her lips and no love in her heart for another who needed help. Perhaps you know her by the name of Provoker, for she was Peninnah the Provoker. I fear there are many such who cross our path today. The one who tries to stir up feelings of anger, jealousy and fretfulness in someone else. One who is filled with her own ways regardless of how she hurts another.

If you know her and have had dealings with her, I expect there have been times when you have said, "Why can't she leave me alone?" But Peninnah can be very persistent and unpleasant. What causes you grief gives her joy! Maybe you have heard her say to someone, "I will take her down a peg or two," or, "I will give her something to think about." There is no end to her provocation, sometimes just pinpricks and at others unbearable.

Maybe you have suffered at her hands, but, on the other hand, I do hope that you are not called by her name. I would not like to think of you as being in her category, but if it should be that you find a resemblance to her in yourself, and your conscience is troubling you because you have deliberately set yourself out to hurt another and have succeeded, then I pray that you will hear the voice of God speaking to you and that your prayer will truly be:

> If I have wounded any soul today,
> If I have caused one foot to go astray,
> If I have walked in my own sinful way,
> Dear Lord, forgive.

Being assured of His forgiveness, please make your way to the one you have hurt and get hers, too. Then sweet will be your peace.

To you, Christian friend, seeking with all your heart to be like your Lord, turn with me for just a moment to Hebrews 10:24, where we read, "Let us consider one another to provoke unto love and to good works." This, then, is the type of Provoker the Lord wants you and me to be! Considerate of others. Seeking to help, feeling for them with sympathy and understanding. Going out of your way to be useful. The kind of provocation permitted to us as

Christians is that which stirs up in the heart of another the things that lead to love and good works. We should call out the very best that is in a person by doing our best for them. Christians have a responsibility to each other and the Lord leaves us in no doubt about it. Let God make you a loving Provoker.

## CRITICISM

"Set a watch, O Lord, before my mouth;
keep the door of my lips." *Psalm 141:3*

ONE day I watched a couple of women in a café having a good old gossip. They were nodding their heads as they whispered to each other in a knowing sort of fashion and were really enjoying themselves. Yet, at the same time they were keeping a furtive look-out. Every now and again they would glance up and look towards the door, then continue their backbiting or whatever it was they were doing!

Suddenly, the door opened and a third person appeared on the scene and silence gripped those two gossipers. With a sickly sort of smile they shook hands with the newcomer. It was evident that she was the subject of their conversation. I had to leave just after that, but, oh dear, I could feel the atmosphere and was sorry for that poor woman who had joined them.

I thought of the time when I had spilled some water on my tablecloth one morning and watched it spread all over in just a few seconds. The damage that was done by just a careless touch to a glass. What about the injury that was possibly done to one woman because of the uncontrolled tongues of the other two!

This was brought home to me very realistically as I read in the Old Testament in the book of Numbers, chapter 12, the story of another woman that we tend to pass by because it is not pleasant reading or because it convicts us of the same sort of thing. We don't like it. Yet, the Word of God is for reproof and rebuke as well as encouragement and exhortation. If we want one, we must accept the other.

We see Miriam looking for a listening ear into which to pour her complaints against her brother Moses. She resented the fact that God was using him and was jealous of what God chose to do. So, instead of standing by the man who had already borne enough, she goes off to Aaron and starts putting her case to him. Anyway, she was annoyed with Moses because he had married a woman that they disapproved of and that started the ball rolling.

Where did it stop? "Does he think that he is the only person that God uses," she says. Let us read verse 2. "And they said, Hath the Lord indeed spoken only by Moses? hath he not spoken also by us? And the Lord heard it." In the bitterness of their jealousy and criticism they had forgotten that God was the silent Listener to what they were saying to each other! But they were soon to find out. The voice of the Lord broke in upon them and called them to account. They were silenced as they listened to God's vindication of His servant, whom He called faithful, and was known as the meekest of men. "Why were you not afraid to speak against my servant Moses? And the anger of the Lord was kindled against them, and He departed."

Miriam has to bear God's judgment, and as she looks at herself she finds she is suddenly a leper. Such was the Lord's drastic way of dealing with one who had given her tongue over to condemn another in a spirit of jealousy. He was God's chosen servant, and touching him was touching something very precious to God.

Now you see the meekness of Moses. He left God to vindicate him, and when Aaron comes pleading and confessing their sin, Moses prays to the Lord for his sister. What grace and pity he showed. "O, Lord," he prays, "I beseech Thee heal her." The effectual fervent prayer of a righteous man availeth much. God shortened the period of her uncleanness. But she was to feel the effects of her slander in herself, and for seven days she had to be shut out from fellowship. They waited for her, however, and did not continue their journey until she was restored to them.

Oh, may we not give our ears to those who would fill them with unkind thoughts about others, nor our tongues to touch the Lord's anointed. These things ought not to be in us as Christians, and the

Lord reminds us of that in James 3:10. "Out of the same mouth
proceedeth blessing and cursing. My brethren, these things ought
not so to be."

Not long ago I read of a woman who had maligned her pastor.
Her lips were soiled with the whisperings she had passed on to many
who believed her. Then she fell ill, and was in such a troubled state
of mind about what she had done that she determined to go and see
him as soon as she could. He welcomed her and listened to her
story as she craved for his forgiveness. Being a man of God, he
forgave her, but felt that she must do something for him. So he
asked her to go home and pluck a chicken and take the feathers and
leave them in various streets and come back to him. Now he said,
"You have done well, but go and gather them all up again". She
looked at him in dismay. "This is impossible," she said, "for the
wind will have scattered them far and wide." He looked at her and
said, "Yes, and that is what happens to our words. Once they are
uttered we cannot take them back again." How true!

Perhaps you find yourself in the same position as Moses. You
are the one being spoken against! Well, see how you can safely
leave the Lord to vindicate you, and deal with the strife of tongues.
He never makes a mistake and His judgments are right.

Miriam's story is not a pleasant one, but it will have been worth
while to us if it makes us pray for each day, "Set a watch, O Lord,
before my mouth; keep the door of my lips."

## SHUT IN

"Thou knowest my downsitting and
mine uprising." *Psalm 139:2*

TODAY, a special word of greeting to those of you who are "shut in".
The number seems to be on the increase. I was surprised the other
day when I was turning over the pages of a small book on my desk
to find three short verses that just seemed to suit your need, so I am
going to share them with you. Here they are:

There was so much that I wanted to do, dear Lord,
  Oh, so much that I wanted to do;
But now, with most of it still undone,
  I am shut in alone with You!

Shut in, but not shut out,
  From the wonderful power of prayer
For on spiritual wings I can still send aid
  To the needy ones everywhere.

And sometimes I think as I finger the key,
  Unlocking Thy promises true,
That perhaps I am filling a far greater need
  Just shut in alone with You.

Isn't that lovely, and isn't that just you? I do not know the author, but it must surely have been someone who like yourself was shut in away from the hustle and bustle of the outside world. Or one who really entered into the feelings of those shut in. Shut in, but not shut out from the most important things in life.

You are housebound for all kinds of reasons, chiefly physical, from arthritis to strokes. Some find themselves among the "shut ins" because they have to attend to the needs of loved ones dependent on their care. Others again feel themselves shut in because there is no place of worship near by where they can enjoy true fellowship.

Yes, I wanted so much just a wee word for you that would bring you some cheer, and the passage that keeps coming to my mind is Psalm 139. It is packed full of reminders that you can never get away from His care! He knows all about you, and just where you live. There can never be any doubt about that, however dark the day may seem.

Look at verse 1 where the Psalmist says, "O Lord, Thou has searched me, and known me." So far as you are concerned, He has looked right down into your heart and knows you even by name. As I said once before, He never mixes you up with someone else. As His redeemed child, you are not just a casual acquaintance, you know, but His in a very special way. You are never out of His thoughts even when the night falls and darkness shuts you in!

Darkness and light are both alike to Him, and He surrounds you. Compassed about.

Life has become restricted for you, measured just in terms of getting up and sitting down, or a few steps now and again. Every movement is known to the Lord your Creator. Says the Psalmist, "Lord, Thou knowest my downsitting and mine uprising." Yes, He knows the feebleness of strength or the pain that accompanies certain movements. He is aware of it all. I heard one of our workers mention this verse the other day, and he said that as he was travelling in the States, he realized in a new way that the Lord knew all of their "ups and downs". How true and how comforting, and He does not scold! So, don't be discouraged, for He understands even your thoughts afar off, thoughts that you can't frame in words. If bed claims most of your day, He is there, too, compassing even your lying down.

He knows all about your thwarted feelings because all of your nicely laid plans have crumbled in the dust. You were always so active running around after other needy folk. Yes, there was so much you wanted to do. There were those tears of frustration before you were able to accept your present situation, but fret not any more, dear friend, for even there in your room God can give you a wonderful ministry and make you a rich blessing in a way you never dreamed of.

I knew a woman, always a shut in; she had never known any other kind of life. But what a ministry of prayer she had. Her bedroom became a place of power and blessing. She made untold friends around the world through letters and visits from missionaries. In spite of much pain, she was always thanking God for the great compensations He had given her. To visit her was to come away blessed. She possessed a peace that very few know anything about, and a quiet radiant face. Oh, yes, His loving kindness is over all His work and I want you to remember that He is round about you in your home or perchance in a hospital. May you know a rich and fruitful experience of the Lord day by day.

And just before we close, a word to those of you who are not shut in. You are enjoying good health and many blessings, don't forget to see if you can lighten the day of someone who is shut in. Those flowers, or that card, or a friendly visit with a word from the

Lord that will encourage and make the day bright. It will help you too, you know!

So may I leave with you all today Psalm 139, and as you read it, I pray that God will give you a real uplift and blessing through it.

## BIRTHDAYS

*"Even to your old age I am he; and even to hoar hairs will I carry you." Isaiah 46: 4*

IT was a birthday party arranged for my husband and, while entering into it all, I found myself quietly thinking about birthdays and realized that under the good hand of God we had much to be thankful for. Then my thoughts strayed away from the present to Psalm 37, where David was giving testimony, not at a birthday party, but looking back on the years that had sped by, and he was able to say, "I have been young, and now am old; yet have I not seen the righteous forsaken, nor his seed begging bread."

I do not know how many milestones he was able to count at that time, but through all the experiences that came his way, the thorns and the briers, the temptations and the testings, the battles and the conquests, blessings and difficulties, he looks back and leaves on record the story of God's faithfulness to him. "I have been young," he says. Yes, he had walked that way, the one that was familiar to youth with all its ups and downs. The years had added up, and through everything he had constantly proved that God was faithful to the trusting soul.

As life went on into maturity, he was ever aware that God was caring for him. In the midst of need and loneliness often, he was satisfied with what God had provided for him. Now as he approaches old age, as some of you are doing, he sits down and remembers. Calls to mind all the way the Lord had led him, not living in the past, but only recounting the wonderful faithfulness of God.

His testimony is one that should help the younger group that follow on. Looking at them, you can almost hear him say, "I have been young, I know the path that you tread and the God who was with me will see you through if you trust Him." What a thrilling testimony! Birthday parties would be different if everyone could give the same response. I am thankful that I have proved through the years that God is faithful, aren't you?

I wonder if today as you read, dear Christian friend, you are conscious of how the years are slipping away. Birthdays seem to have a way of coming round so quickly. Maybe there is just a wee bit of anxiety in your heart as you contemplate the future. You don't know what it has in store for you and you wonder how you will make out. Let David's assurance encourage you and then read with me that very precious verse found in Isaiah 46:4. The Lord says, "Even to your old age I am he, and even to hoar hairs will I carry you: I have made, and I will bear; even I will carry, and will deliver you."

There is assurance for the past, the present and the future. Right down through the years to old age "I am with you". Why spoil the blessing of today by worrying about what is going to happen tomorrow when He says, "I will take care of you"? He will never let you down and even when your hair is turning grey and there is less of it, you have His promise upon which you can depend.

I know that things may get more difficult for you as the years go by. And He knows that too, and will walk beside you, the most faithful friend you have ever known. He will do better for you than you could ever do for yourself, for His ways are past finding out. I love to remind myself that God is not limited as we are! "Yes," said David, "my whole life long I have seen God do things for me." Young, and now I am old, but I have never seen a trusting soul left desolate or empty!

Just in case you are tempted to think that there is nothing left for you to do, and you find it a bit irksome after having been once so active, turn to Psalm 92 and read it through, especially the last verse. Speaking of righteous ones, the Psalmist says, "They shall still bring forth fruit in old age; they shall be fat and flourishing." That is not a picture of wilting away, but just the opposite. The woman who has walked along life's way with the Lord in control will have a rich experience which will not cease with advancing years. Hers is the life that can still shine and radiate blessing.

Let the future be in the hands of God, as we read together the verse of that lovely old hymn which says:

> Even down to old age my people shall prove,
> My sovereign, eternal, unchangeable love;
> And then, when grey hairs shall their temples adorn,
> Like lambs shall they still in my bosom be borne.